W9-ACA-412

First Grade

Everyday Mathematics®

Assessment Handbook

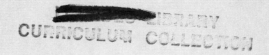

First Grade

Everyday Mathematics®

Assessment Handbook

**The University of Chicago
School Mathematics Project**

 **Wright Group**

The McGraw·Hill Companies

UCSMP Elementary Materials Component

Max Bell, Director

Authors
Jean Bell
William M. Carroll

Photo Credits
Page 8, Phil Martin/Photography
Cover: Bill Burlingham/Photography
Photo Collage: Herman Adler Design

Acknowledgments
We gratefully acknowledge the work of the following classroom teachers
who provided input and suggestions as we designedthis handbook:
Huong Bahn, Fran Moore, Jenny Waters, and Lana Winnet.

Contributors
Ellen Dairyko, Sharon Draznin, Nancy Hanvey, Laurie Leff, Denise Porter
Herb Price, Joyce Timmons, Lisa Winters

Printed in the United States of America.

Send all inquiries to:
Wright Group/McGraw-Hill
P.O. Box 812960
Chicago, IL 60681

ISBN 0-07-584447-8

7 8 9 POH 09 08 07 06 05

Contents

Introduction

Too often, school assessment is equated with testing and grading. While some formal assessment is necessary, it tends to provide only scattered snapshots of children rather than records of their growth and progress. The philosophy of *Everyday Mathematics*® is that real assessment should be more like a motion picture revealing the development of the child's mathematical understanding while giving the teacher useful feedback about instructional needs. Rather than simply providing tests on isolated skills, *Everyday Mathematics* offers a variety of useful techniques and opportunities to assess children's progress on skills, concepts, and thinking processes.

Several assessment tools are built into the *Everyday Mathematics* program. Slate assessments and end-of-unit written assessments are useful in showing how well students are learning the concepts and skills covered in a unit. But these tools by themselves do not provide a balance, highlight progress, or show children's work on larger problems. The purpose of this handbook is to broaden your assessment techniques. Rather than using all of the techniques suggested here, choose a few that balance written work with observation, individual work with group work, and short answers with longer explanations.

For assessment to be valid and useful to both teachers and children, the authors believe that

- teachers need to have a variety of assessment tools and techniques from which to choose.

- children should be included in the assessment process through interviews, written work, and conferences that provide appropriate feedback. Self-assessment and reflection are skills that will develop over time if encouraged.

- assessment and instruction should be closely linked. Assessment should assist teachers in making instructional decisions concerning both individual children and the whole class.

- a good assessment plan makes instruction easier.

- the best assessment plans are those developed by teachers working collaboratively within their schools.

This handbook compiles classroom-tested techniques used by experienced *Everyday Mathematics* teachers. It includes suggestions for observing students, keeping anecdotal records, following student progress, and encouraging children to reflect on and communicate both what they have learned and how they feel about mathematics. Many of the assessment suggestions are aimed specifically at *Everyday Mathematics* activities, such as using Explorations to observe students or using Math Boxes to focus on a particular concept or skill.

As you read through this handbook, you may want to start with one or two activities that fit your needs and assist you in building a balanced approach to assessment. Feel free to adapt the materials to your own needs. While some teachers find Math Logs useful, others find observations and short, informal interviews more helpful, especially when a child is beginning first grade.

The *Everyday Mathematics* goal is to furnish you with some ideas to make assessment and instruction more manageable, productive, and exciting as well as offer you a more complete picture of each child's progress and instructional needs.

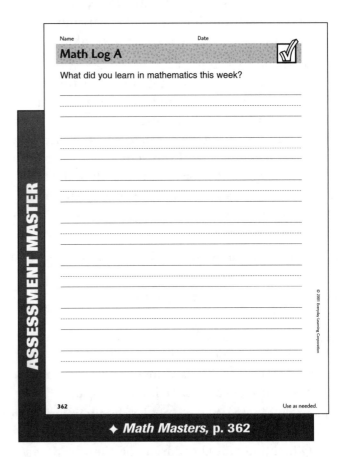

◆ *Math Masters, p. 362*

A Balance of Assessments

Although there is no one "right" assessment plan for all classrooms, all assessment plans should use a variety of techniques. To develop your own plan, consider four different assessment sources within the Quad shown in the figure below. The content of this handbook provides further details about these sources. The section beginning on page 35 provides examples for each unit of how to use different types of assessments in specific lessons.

Ongoing, Product, and Periodic Assessments, and Outside Tests

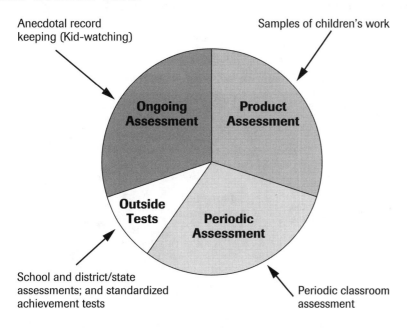

Anecdotal record keeping (Kid-watching)

Samples of children's work

Ongoing Assessment

Product Assessment

Outside Tests

Periodic Assessment

School and district/state assessments; and standardized achievement tests

Periodic classroom assessment

Ongoing Assessment includes observations of children as they are working on regular classroom activities, in groups during Explorations and games, or independently on Math Boxes. It also may include children's thinking and shared strategies as well as information you gather from classroom interactions or brief, informal, individual interviews. Records of these ongoing assessments may take the form of short written notes, more elaborate record sheets, or brief mental notes to yourself. See Ongoing Assessment, pages 13–17, for details.

Product Assessment may include samples of daily written work; group project reports; and mathematical writing, drawing, sketches, diagrams, or anything else you feel has value and reflects what you want children to learn. If you are keeping portfolios, children should help select which products to include in them. See Portfolios, pages 7–10, and Product Assessment, pages 19–22.

Periodic Assessment includes more formal assessments, such as end-of-unit assessments, quizzes, Progress Indicators, and Math Interest Inventories. Pages 23–30 offer suggestions and extensions intended to help you measure both individual and class progress using these types of assessment.

Outside Tests provide information from school, district, state, or standardized tests that might be used to evaluate the progress of a child, class, or school. See pages 31 and 32 for more information.

The types of assessment sources used within the Quad are quite flexible and depend on a number of factors, such as grade level, children's experience, time of year, and so on. For example, Kindergarten and first grade teachers, especially at the beginning of the year, probably use more of the material from the Ongoing Assessment source and less from Product and Periodic Assessment sources. In contrast, teachers in higher grades may rely more on the Product, Periodic, and Outside Assessment sources.

Flexible Quad Proportions

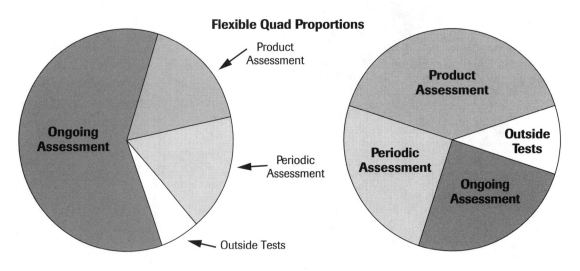

Possible First Grade Proportions   Possible Third Grade Proportions

A List of Assessment Sources attached to children's folders or portfolios or in your record book may help you see whether you have included information from the first three sources of the Quad as well as from other sources. Notice that the completed sample shown below includes only a few of the assessment suggestions from each source. Another teacher might choose other entries. Using multiple techniques will give you a clear picture of each child's progress and instructional needs.

Use this List of Assessment Sources master to keep track of the assessment sources that you are currently using. A blank sample is provided as *Math Masters,* page 354. The Assessment Masters, included at the back of your *Math Masters* book, are shown in reduced form on pages 66–99 of this book.

NOTE: Do not try to use all assessment sources at once. Instead, devise a manageable, balanced plan.

Your assessment plan should answer these questions:

- *How is the class performing as a whole?*
- *How are individual children performing?*
- *How can I adjust instruction to meet children's needs?*
- *How can I communicate to children, parents, and others about the progress being made?*

Your Assessment Ideas

_____

_____

_____

_____

_____

_____

_____

_____

_____

_____

_____

_____

_____

_____

_____

_____

_____

_____

_____

_____

_____

_____

_____

_____

_____

Portfolios

Using Portfolios

Portfolios are used for a number of different purposes, from keeping track of progress to helping children become more reflective about their mathematical growth. Because many schools, districts, and states are developing their own guidelines and requirements for portfolios, the *Everyday Mathematics* authors are reluctant to make specific suggestions. However, there are several reasons that the practice of keeping portfolios is positive and consistent with the philosophy of *Everyday Mathematics:*

- Portfolios emphasize progress over time, rather than results at a given moment. At any time, a child may have Beginning, Developing, or Secure understandings of various mathematical concepts. This progress can best be exhibited by a collection of products organized into portfolios or folders that contain work from different contexts and from different times in the year.

- Portfolios can involve children more directly in the assessment process. Children may write introductions and help select portfolio entries. They can select work they are especially proud of and tag each piece with an explanation of why it was chosen. The margin sample shows how a child might use self-assessment forms to tag and evaluate a piece of work. Children may need guidance in developing realistic self-assessment, which is a valuable skill that takes time to develop. Blank self-assessment forms (My Work) are provided in *Math Masters,* pages 365 and 366.

- Portfolios can be used as evidence of progress for children, their families, and their teachers for next year. You may want to establish a "Portfolio Night" for children and their parents to attend in order to allow them time to discuss and review the contents. It is very important that parents understand the goals of the various projects and assignments.

- Portfolios can illustrate children's strengths and weaknesses in particular areas of mathematics. Since a rich body of work can be contained in a portfolio, it is a good vehicle for exhibiting each child's progress. It also can be used to assess children's abilities to see connections within mathematics and to apply mathematical ideas to real-world situations.

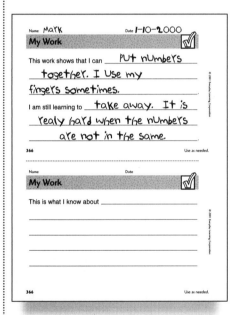

Some teachers keep two types of portfolios: a working portfolio in which students store their recent work and an assessment portfolio. Occasionally, a selection of work is transferred from the working portfolio to the assessment portfolio. Usually, the teacher provides some guidelines for what should be selected, allowing children to choose within these guidelines.

Many teachers recommend that the number of mathematics entries in an assessment portfolio be kept to a limited number. These entries provide a manageable but representative sample of work. New work can replace old, but some samples from throughout the year should remain.

Listed below are some ideas of representative work that might be included in a portfolio:

• Projects in progress and in completed form

• Children's solutions to challenging problems
• Written accounts of children's feelings about mathematics
• Drawings, sketches, and representations of mathematical ideas and situations
• Photographs of children interacting with manipulatives
• Photographs of children working individually and in groups
• Videos portraying children communicating mathematically

For more guidance on developing portfolio assessment, you may wish to consult one of several excellent sources listed on page 33 of this handbook. We especially recommend *Mathematics Assessment: Myths, Models, Good Questions, and Practical Suggestions,* edited by Jean Kerr Stenmark, available through the National Council of Teachers of Mathematics (NCTM). Portfolios, as well as other assessment issues, are also frequently addressed in the NCTM journal *Teaching Children Mathematics.* A video available from NCTM, *Mathematics Assessment: Alternative Approaches,* also discusses portfolios and may be helpful for teachers who are working together to develop a schoolwide assessment policy.

Ideas in the *Teacher's Lesson Guide*

Portfolio Ideas Samples of children's work may be obtained from the following assignments:

Unit 1

- Drawing Portraits (**Lesson 1.1**)
- Reviewing the Meaning of Mathematics (**Lesson 1.2**)
- Making Geometric Designs (**Lesson 1.3**)
- Writing the Numbers 1 and 2 (**Lesson 1.5**)
- Writing the Numbers 3 and 4 (**Lesson 1.8**)
- Writing the Numbers 5 and 6 (**Lesson 1.10**)
- Writing the Numbers 1 through 6 (**Lessons 1.11 and 1.13**)
- Making a Weather Activity Booklet (**Lesson 1.12**)
- Play *Top-It* (**Lesson 1.14**)

Unit 2

- Practicing 7s and 8s (**Lesson 2.3**)
- Practicing 9s and 0s (**Lesson 2.5**)
- Telling Time (**Lesson 2.13**)
- Play *Two-Fisted Penny Addition* (**Lesson 2.14**)
- Find 2-Addend Combinations for Sums of 10 (**Lesson 2.14**)

Unit 3

- Exchanging Coins (**Lesson 3.11**)
- Identify and Complete Patterns (**Lesson 3.15**)

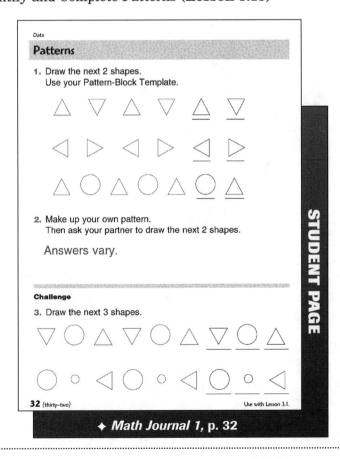

♦ *Math Journal 1*, p. 32

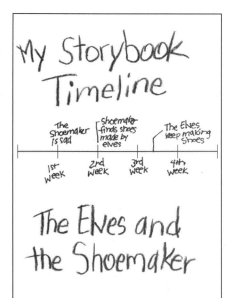

Unit 4
- Reading a Thermometer (**Lesson 4.1**)
- Making a Storybook Timeline (**Lesson 4.9**)
- Draw Domino Number Families (**Lesson 4.11**)

Unit 5
- Making a Classroom Number-Story Book (**Lesson 5.8**)
- Solving "What's My Rule?" Problems (**Lesson 5.13**)

Unit 6
- Finding the Relationships Among Pattern Blocks (**Lesson 6.7**)
- Writing Timing Me Number Stories (**Lesson 6.11**)
- Solve Name-Collection Box Problems (**Lesson 6.13**)

Unit 7
- Making Attribute-Block Designs (**Lesson 7.2**)
- Building and Drawing a Pattern-Block Design (**Lesson 7.3**)
- Playing the *Tens-and-Ones Trading Game* (**Lesson 7.5**)
- Draw a Picture with 2-Dimensional Shapes (**Lesson 7.8**)
- Find Symmetry (**Lesson 7.8**)

Unit 8
- Playing with a Dollar Bill (**Lesson 8.5**)
- Making a Fraction Book (**Lesson 8.7**)
- Making Fraction Creatures (**Lesson 8.8**)

- Recording and Identifying Pattern-Block Shapes (**Lesson 8.9**)
- Finding Relationships Involving Pattern Blocks (**Lesson 8.9**)

Unit 9
- Making a Class Number-Story Book (**Lesson 9.4**)
- Comparing Fractions (**Lesson 9.7**)
- Finding Fraction Combinations Equivalent to $\frac{1}{2}$ (**Lesson 9.8**)

Rubrics

One good way to keep track of each child's progress is to use a rubric. A rubric is a framework that helps you categorize progress on various aspects of a child's learning. A simple but effective rubric that many teachers use is the classification of children as Beginning, Developing, or Secure with respect to a particular skill or concept. This is illustrated below.

Sample Rubric

Beginning (B)
Children cannot complete the task independently. They show little understanding of the concept or skill.

Developing (D)
Children show some understanding. However, errors or misunderstandings still occur. Reminders, hints, and suggestions are needed to promote children's understanding.

Secure (S)
Children can apply the skill or concept correctly and independently.

This simple rubric can be easily used with any of the sample assessment tools to keep track of the progress of individual children as well as the whole class. You may wish to use B, D, and S or another set of symbols, such as −, ✓, and +; Levels C, B, and A; or some other rubric symbols you prefer. One teacher suggests using red, yellow, and green color symbols.

No matter which rubric symbols you use, you can take a quick look at a completed Class Checklist or a Class Progress Indicator to see which areas need further review or which children will benefit from additional help or challenge.

Because some children fall between Developing and Secure or may show exemplary understanding, a 3-point rubric may seem insufficient for some areas you wish to assess. This may be especially true when you are examining performance on a Project or other larger activity. A general five-level rubric follows on the next page.

Class Progress Indicator

Mathematical Topic Being Assessed: _____

	BEGINNING	DEVELOPING OR DEVELOPING+	SECURE OR SECURE+
First Assessment After Lesson: ___ Dates included: ___ to ___			
Second Assessment After Lesson: ___ Dates included: ___ to ___			
Third Assessment After Lesson: ___ Dates included: ___ to ___			

Notes
_____
_____
_____

◆ Math Masters, p. 358

ASSESSMENT MASTER

Sample Rubric

Beginning (B)
Children's responses may have fragments of appropriate material and may show effort to accomplish the task. However, the responses indicate little understanding of either the concepts or computational procedure involved.

Developing (D)
Children are not ready to revise their responses without conversation or more teaching. Part of the task is accomplished, but it is apparent that more understanding is needed in order for children to accomplish the entire task.

Developing+ (D+)
Responses convince you that children can revise their work in order to achieve a Secure performance with the help of feedback (in other words, teacher prompts). While understanding is good, it is not quite Secure or completely independent.

Secure (S)
Children's strategies and executions meet the content, thinking processes, and demands of the task. The responses reflect a broad range of understanding, and children can apply the understanding in different contexts.

Secure+ (S+)
A Secure+ performance is exciting. In addition to meeting the qualifications for Secure, it also merits distinction for special insights, good communication and reasoning, or other exceptional qualities.

NOTE: These rubrics are provided as an introduction to the general topic of rubrics. The most effective rubrics will be ones that you and your fellow grade-level teachers tailor to the needs of your children, as well as to the content you are teaching.

Remember, the rubrics are only a framework. When you wish to use a rubric, general indicators should be made more specific to fit the task, the time of the year, and the grade level at which the rubric is being used. Some examples of rubrics applied to specific tasks are illustrated in this handbook in the section on Progress Indicators/Performance Indicators beginning on page 24.

Finally, another example of a general rubric is given below. This rubric might be applied to a problem in which children are asked both to find an answer and to explain (or illustrate) their reasoning. Rubrics like these can be used to assess not only individual performance on an extended problem, but also group processes on problem-solving tasks.

Sample Rubric

Level 0
No attempts are made to solve the problem.

Level 1
Partial attempts are made. Reasoning is not explained. Problems are misunderstood, or little progress is made.

Level 2
Children arrive at solutions, and children clearly show reasoning and correct processes, but solutions are incorrect.
or:
Solutions are correct with little or no explanation given.

Level 3
Solutions are correct. Explanations are attempted but are incomplete.

Level 4
Solutions are correct. Explanations are clear and complete.

Level 5
Children offer exemplary solutions.

Ongoing Assessment

Observation of children during regular classroom interactions, as they work independently or in groups, is an important assessment technique in *Everyday Mathematics*. The following suggestions may help you manage and record these ongoing observations.

Recording Tools

Flip-Card Collection

Some teachers have found it helpful to attach index cards to a clipboard for recording observations. To do this, use one card for each child. You can use one color for the first five children, a second color for the next five children, and so on. Focus on one set of five each day, along with any other anecdotal observations from the rest of the children. Try to observe each child at least once every two weeks. Be sure to date your observations so that you can track improvements.

After a child's index card has become filled with information, remove it and file it alphabetically. Tape a new card to the clipboard to repeat the process.

The completed cards will help you keep track of children's needs and the implications for instruction. They are also useful for preparing for parent conferences.

Seating Charts or Calendar Grids

Place each child's name in one of the grid cells and write observations in the cells as you circulate throughout the classroom. After reflecting on whole-class needs, cut apart the cells, date them, and file them for each child. Use them to analyze individual strengths and needs and to prepare for parent conferences.

Computer Labels

Print out children's names on sheets of large computer address labels. Write observations on the appropriate labels. As labels become filled, place them on cards or in a notebook for individual children.

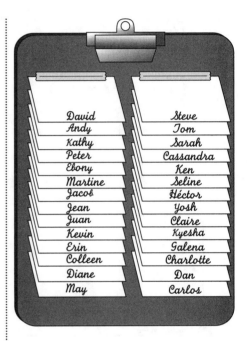

NOTE: Sequentially number the reviewed cards for each child so you can easily see children who may have been missed (for example, you might notice that you are on Card #3 for most of the children and still on Card #1 for a few).

Observational Class Checklists

A blank checklist is provided on *Math Masters,* page 356. You may want to use it for recording ongoing observations and interactions.

So that you won't have to rewrite children's names on each checklist you use, make a copy of the blank checklist. On the copy, list the names of your children, perhaps by the groups you wish to assess at any one time. This will be your "Class Checklist" from which additional copies can be made. List the learning goals you are currently teaching and wish to assess.

The blank "Names" Master (*Math Masters,* page 357) is provided so that, if necessary, you can change the order of children's names on subsequent "Class Checklists" or on any of the grade-level checklists referred to in this handbook.

One teacher suggests attaching a blank Class Checklist to the back of a flip-card clipboard or a similar ongoing recording device and then identifying a particular concept or skill and using a rubric symbol on the checklist to indicate students' progress. (See information on Rubrics, pages 11 and 12.) Blank cells can show which children to focus on the next time you revisit the topic. The checklist indicates which children or which topics should require additional attention.

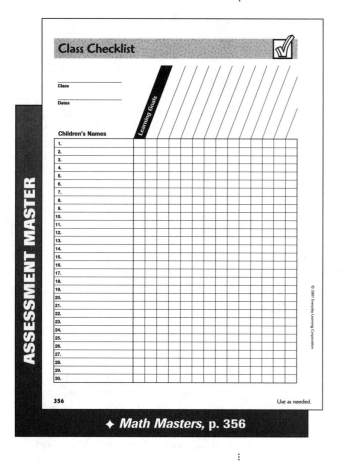

♦ *Math Masters, p. 356*

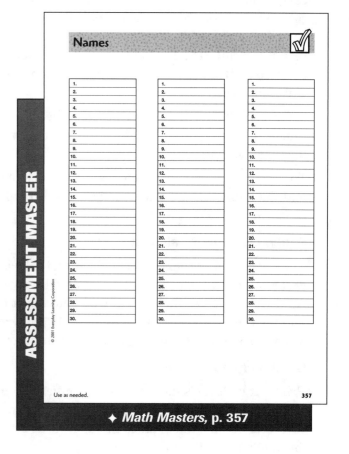

♦ *Math Masters, p. 357*

Math Box Cover-Up

Some teachers use Math Boxes to assess progress. The scenario below is from an *Everyday Mathematics* teacher.

One Teacher's Use of Math Boxes

Much of the assessment in Ms. Summers' third grade classroom is ongoing observation—short notes on progress made as children work on an activity. Generally, children are unaware that they are being assessed. For example, as children are working on a set of Math Boxes, Ms. Summers has a copy of the day's Math Boxes page attached to her clipboard and has identified particular cells that she would like to assess. These identified cells are covered with self-stick notes.

As she circulates through the classroom, Ms. Summers observes children's performance on these targeted cells. If a child is having difficulty with a particular cell, Ms. Summers may ask a probing question or two. If appropriate, the child's name is recorded on that self-stick note, sometimes with a note about the particular difficulty the child seemed to be having.

Ms. Summers may also indicate the progress that she sees various children making, as well as the names of those who need extended challenges.

Later, Ms. Summers works with those children who need additional review, either individually or in a small group.

In sum, Ms. Summers uses Math Boxes to reinforce, review, and extend particular skills and concepts. If a particular concept is troublesome for the class, it will be revisited in future lessons and Math Boxes.

Ms. Summers also uses Math Boxes to communicate with parents and guardians about the mathematics being taught in the classroom and about individual children's strengths and weaknesses. Along with her observational notes, Ms. Summers finds Math Boxes to be a useful tool for assessing the progress both of her class and of individual children.

Using Recording Tools

Finding time to use the recording tools suggested in the previous section is important. Choose the one that appeals to you most and try it. If necessary, adapt it to make it more useful to you, or try another tool. Listed below are some *Everyday Mathematics* approaches and routines, with suggestions on ways to use recording tools.

Teacher-Guided Instruction

During the lesson, circulate around the room, interacting with children and observing the mathematical behavior that is taking place. Identify those children who are having difficulty as well as those who are showing progress. Be alert to significant comments and interactions. These quick observations often tell a great deal about a child's mathematical thinking. Practice making mental notes on the spot, and follow them up with brief written notes when possible. The important thing is to find an efficient way to keep track of children's progress without getting overwhelmed with papers, lists, and notes.

Mathematical Mini-Interviews

Observing and listening to children as they work will enable you to note progress. However, there are times when brief oral interactions with probing questions clarify and enhance observations. These brief, nonthreatening, one-on-one interactions overheard by the rest of the class or in private, as appropriate, encourage mathematical communication skills. They should, however, apply to the content at hand. For example, when children are counting as a group, you may ask some of them, "Let's see how high you can count by 5s." Or, when children are explaining addition strategies, you can ask, "What are the units for this number story?"

Games

At the beginning of the year, when children are first becoming comfortable with the games and are playing them in small groups, move around the classroom observing the strategies that children are employing. Once children are playing the games independently, assemble a small group of those having difficulty with Math Boxes cells, computational strategies, or other related problem areas and provide help to them. Use the recording tools to note any valuable information regarding individual mathematical development. You can also use this time to conduct mathematical mini-interviews.

Mental Math and Reflexes

As you present the class with Mental Math and Reflexes situations, focus on a small core group of children. For example, you might start with the first five children on the clipboard or grid. You should never feel that all children need to be observed every day.

Strategy Sharing

Over time, encourage each child to share his or her strategies while working at the board or overhead projector. It is during this time that you should assume the role of "guide on the side" rather than "sage on the stage." Record which strategies the child uses. In the *Everyday Mathematics* classroom, many strategies are being utilized; recording children's strategies will help you know how to address individual strengths and needs. You will also have an opportunity to consider communication skills and processes as well as answers.

Explorations

During Explorations lessons, you can observe children participating in manipulative-based activities. As children work in small groups, you may wish to observe specific children. Another option is to establish your own workstation. As you guide children through an Exploration, note the processes, the verbalization, and the thinking that are taking place.

Slates

Periodically, record children's responses from their slate reviews. You may want to focus on one group at a time and indicate only those children with Beginning understanding. Provide follow-up instruction for them based on your notes.

Your Assessment Ideas

Product Assessment

Samples of children's mathematical writings, drawing, and creations add breadth to the assessment process. In this section, we offer suggestions and other sources for product assessment and review some of the products that are part of *Everyday Mathematics*. Some of these items can be selected and stored in a portfolio or work folder along with other assessments.

Products from *Everyday Mathematics*

Math Boxes

Math Boxes provide quick glimpses into how a child performs in several areas. As suggested in the Ongoing Assessment section of this book, they can also be adapted to assess topics of concern. You may find it useful to check two or three specific items that repeat throughout the year, such as Frames and Arrows or "What's My Rule?" tables.

Math Journals

Math Journals can be considered working portfolios. Children should keep the journals intact so that they can revisit, review, correct, and improve their responses at a later time. You or children might select journal pages focusing on topics of concern or number stories featuring "do your own" exercises to photocopy and include in portfolios.

Math Masters

Math Masters, such as Home Links, may be collected or copied (in the case of the personal data pages) and used for product assessment. Although Home Links are less useful for assessing children because of home differences, they *can* be used to initiate discussion at parent conferences. Some teachers work on the Home Links with children in class and then send them home for discussion.

Explorations and Projects

Some of the Explorations and Projects generate 3-dimensional products that are either transitional or permanent. Displays, the use of a Polaroid camera, or brief videos can be helpful in capturing some of these products.

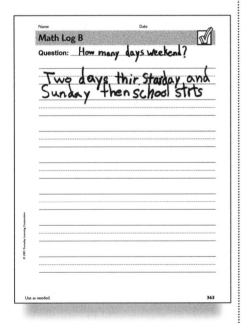

Additional Assessment Products

Many teachers are interested in gathering examples of children's writing and thinking in addition to those provided by *Everyday Mathematics* materials. This type of writing is usually more open-ended and provides children with opportunities to reflect, assess their understanding, and enhance their communication skills. This section offers examples of products you may want to include in your assessment plan.

Math Logs and Alternatives

Some teachers find it beneficial for children to write about mathematics regularly. A spiral notebook or a set of log sheets can be used as a Math Log. (See sample masters on *Math Masters*, pages 362–364.) Children may use the back side of Math Log sheets to draw a picture to illustrate what they learned. Not only can these written reflections serve as a powerful means of checking children's understanding, but they are also a means of assessing curiosity, persistence, and self-confidence.

Remember that Math Logs are not "end products" but, instead, are an important part of the ongoing assessment process referred to on page 3. They are helpful to both you and children only if they reveal useful information and encourage the development of mathematical thinking, understanding, and written communication. Here are some suggestions on how to get children writing:

Open-Ended Questions Use open-ended questions to start children writing. Some prompts that you can use are:

• *Why is (this answer) right or wrong? Explain.*
• *What was your strategy for finding the answer?*
• *How many ways can you find an answer for this problem?*
• *How is this like something you have learned before?*

Children may use My Exit Slip sheets to record responses to open-ended questions at the close of a lesson or unit. (See *Math Masters,* page 367.)

Number Stories Occasionally ask children to write and/or draw a number story. Sometimes, you may wish to supply the numbers. For example:

• *Write a number story that uses the numbers 8 and 5.*

At other times, you may leave the instructions more open-ended:

• *Make up a number story using large numbers.*
• *Write or draw a number story that shows addition.*

Written number stories provide concrete assessment of children's understanding of operations, relationships, and numbers. For example, many children confuse addition situations with subtraction situations. Number stories often point out misconceptions.

Portfolio Writing If you are using portfolios, children can write or dictate entries for their portfolios to show what they know about numbers and mathematics. Children might dictate their ideas to you or to a classroom aide. Provide prompts like the following to encourage children to show what they already know:

- *How high you can count?*
- *Write some numbers you know.*
- *Which numbers say something about you? Can you write how old you are? Can you write your address?*

As the year continues, ask children to look at their first entries and to update what they have learned about numbers and mathematics.

Concept and Strategy Writing Prior to the teaching of a unit, invite children to share what they already know about the concepts being presented. For example, before you teach a unit on geometry, children could reflect in response to the following prompts:

- *Which shapes do you know? Name or draw shapes you know.*
- *Look around the room and find shapes that you know. Draw pictures of things you see that have these shapes.*

Children's reflections may help you plan your instruction. At the close of each unit, ask children to respond to the same statements or questions. This allows both you and the children to compare growth in understanding of the concepts.

Later in the year, children can begin to use words, pictures, or both to explain strategies they used to solve problems. Communicating about mathematics encourages children to reflect upon their thinking and provides you with another perspective on the strategies children use. Ask a question and encourage children to write ways for solving the problem. Model this for the children.

I see a clock
a clock is a circle

A cat weighs 7 lbs. A rabbit weighs 6 lbs.
How can you figure out what they weigh together?

I start at 7
on the number
line I hop 6
times I stop
at 13

6 + 13

This is easy. I know
that 6 + 3 = 9

The 1 means there's
10 more.

10 + 9 is 19

What I Like Best
    Playing Top it and
        Penny Grab
What I Need to Practice
    Whats My Rule
    Number Stories

NOTE: How often should you use a Math Log or other writing in math? The answer to this question depends on you and your children. In first grade, you may find that once a week (perhaps on Friday, reflecting on what children did that week) or at the end of the unit is sufficient.

Choose the amount of additional writing with which you and your children feel comfortable.

If you do not want to have children keep regular Math Logs, ask them to occasionally write about mathematics so that they can develop this skill. Once every unit, give children short writing assignments. Ideas can come from any of the Math Log suggestions mentioned previously in this section. These can be given in the form of a Math Message.

Children's Reflections and Self-Assessment

Try to include children in the assessment process. The products listed below will encourage children to develop their ability to think reflectively. These products can be used as Math Messages or Home Links within the program, in Math Logs, or as alternatives to Math Logs.

Open-ended questions, such as those suggested below, provide children with opportunities to reflect on what they know and what they do not know. Invite children to reflect before, during, and/or after a lesson.

Math Masters, pages 362–367 provide alternative formats offered by experienced *Everyday Mathematics* teachers. "My Exit Slips" are suggested for responses to appropriate open-ended questions at the end of a lesson or a unit. Here are some prompts you can use:

- *Tomorrow I want to learn...*
- *I was surprised that I...*
- *I was happy that...*
- *I don't understand...*
- *The most important thing I learned today (this week) is...*
- *I think big numbers are...*
- *What I like most about mathematics is...*
- *What will you tell your family you learned today?*
- *What was the hardest (easiest) part of today's lesson?*
- *What did you like (or not like) about today's lesson?*

Sometimes you may want children to focus on how mathematics games were played in their groups:

- *Which game did you play in your group today?*
- *Which game would your group like to play again?*
- *What do you like or dislike about playing a game in a group?*
- *Did you have problems playing a game with your group? How did you solve these problems?*
- *Does your group need to make new rules for playing together?*

This kind of writing may give teachers some ideas about children's attitudes toward mathematics and about which experiences have been the most beneficial. Responses will vary, depending on the writing and reflective experiences of children.

Periodic Assessment

Periodic assessment activities are those that are done at fairly consistent times or intervals over the school year. We will briefly review periodic assessment sources that are currently part of *Everyday Mathematics* and then discuss additional sources that experienced teachers use.

Sources from *Everyday Mathematics*

Unit Reviews and Assessments

Each unit of your *Teacher's Lesson Guide* ends with a review and assessment lesson that lists the learning goals for that unit. The goals list is followed by a cumulative review that includes suggestions for oral and slate assessments as well as a list of the written assessment items from the Checking Progress Assessment Masters for the unit. And each of these written assessment items is matched to one or more of the learning goals.

This cumulative oral, slate, and written review provides an opportunity for you to check children's progress on concepts and skills that were introduced or further developed in the unit.

Some additional reminders:

- Use rubrics to record children's progress toward each learning goal you assess. Rubrics are introduced on pages 11 and 12 of this book, and examples of how to use them are provided on pages 23–27 and in the Assessment Overview section beginning on page 35.
- Only concepts and skills that are the focus of several activities within any given unit are suggested for assessment at the end of a unit. However, feel free to add concepts and skills that you particularly want to assess or skills from previous units that you wish to reassess.
- Since many of the end-of-unit reviews and assessments tend to focus on skills, you may want to add more conceptual and open-ended questions as suggested in the Product Assessment section of this book, beginning on page 19.

> NOTE: If needed, generate your own reviews and quizzes for periodic review and assessment.
>
> Please give us feedback on your review and assessment ideas; this information may be beneficial to other teachers.

Math Boxes and other *Math Journal* Pages

You can use rubrics to periodically assess Math Boxes and other *Math Journal* pages as independent reviews. By recording appropriate rubric symbols on a Class Progress Indicator (see page margin) or a Class Checklist, you can ascertain which children may need additional experience and perhaps pair or group them with children who offer Secure responses.

Midyear and End-of-Year Assessments

The Midyear and End-of-Year Assessment Masters (*Math Masters,* pages 318–327) provide additional assessment opportunities that you may wish to use as part of your balanced assessment plan. Minis of these masters, with answers, are shown on pages 73–78 of this book. These tests cover important concepts and skills presented in *First Grade Everyday Mathematics,* but they are not designed to be used as "pre-tests" and they should not be your primary assessment tools. Use them along with the ongoing, product, and periodic assessments that are found within the lessons and at the end of each unit.

Additional Sources

Progress Indicators/Performance Indicators

Class Progress Indicators, also known as Performance Indicators, are another assessment tool that some teachers have found useful in assessing and tracking children's progress on selected mathematical topics. For example, early in first grade, you would expect most students to be Beginning or Developing when telling or writing complete number stories. However, by spring, many children will be Secure, and the rest should be Developing. Progress of the whole class, as well as individual children, can be assessed periodically, and appropriate instruction planned accordingly.

A Class Progress Indicator form provides space to record children's performance on any mathematical topic you choose to assess two or three times during the year.

The first assessment opportunity, usually after children have some exposure to and experience with a topic, provides a baseline for your children's performance early in the year. By recording the second and third assessments on the same form, you can track the progress of each child as well as the whole class throughout the school year. A first grade teacher's sample Class Progress Indicator for Frames and Arrows is shown in the margin. A blank form of this master is provided in *Math Masters,* page 358.

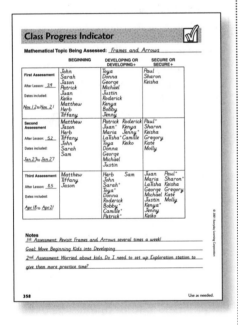

Record the names of children under the columns that most appropriately indicate their levels: Beginning, Developing, or Secure (or whichever rubric symbols you want to use). If you wish, use a plus symbol (+) to indicate children who are between the given levels. As you conduct your assessments, keep this question in mind: *What do I need to do instructionally to promote progress?* Space is provided at the bottom of the form for any notes you may wish to make.

You may adapt the general rubric (Beginning, Developing, Developing+, Secure, Secure+) to your particular class level. Below and on the pages that follow, we offer examples for two mathematical topics. For each of these topics, suggested assessment times are provided, along with specific rubrics. Use the rubric provided or feel free to adapt one to your own class. A blank rubric form is provided on page 360 of *Math Masters*. Use the Class Progress Indicator to assess other topics (such as Frames and Arrows, Numeration, and so on). However, do not assess more than two or three topics the first time through.

The teachers who prepared the following examples reported that creating these specific topic rubrics was not an easy task. Collaborating with colleagues proved helpful. The process takes time, but it becomes easier and is well worth the effort.

Example 1: Number Stories

Number stories assist children in understanding operations and relations, modeling problems, performing mental and written arithmetic, and developing and sharing mathematical language. Number stories are a routine in *Everyday Mathematics* from Kindergarten through grade 3.

Time Frame: Use with or after Lessons 2.13, 5.8, and 8.4.

Number stories are introduced in Lesson 1.13. Assess children sometime after Lesson 2.13, by which time they will have had opportunities to practice and become comfortable with sharing their thoughts and strategies. You may use journal pages 28 and 29 for this first assessment. Or have children draw a simple number story and then dictate it to you.

The second assessment may be done after Lesson 5.8. By this time, children will have had opportunities to tell, draw, write, and solve their number stories. Use the number story that they record on journal page 113 or have them record it on a piece of paper that you can collect. Grade 1, Assessment Master A is provided in *Math Masters*, page 368 for your use.

The third assessment may come after Lesson 8.4. You may use journal page 185, or have children generate their own number stories using the school store posters on journal pages 186 and 187. Use Grade 1 Assessment Master A. The examples shown on the next page for each progress level are from midyear.

NOTE: Ideally, a group of grade-level teachers should go through the same assessments using a B, D, S rubric. Comparing the results and discussing differences, they should arrive at a consensus and record the results to form an appropriate rubric for the topic being assessed, at least to begin with.

NOTE: The time frames are intended only to provide some guidance for when to assess children. Feel free to adjust these times to fit your schedule.

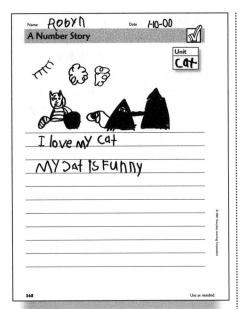

Beginning (B)

Sample Number-Story Rubric

Use a plus symbol (+) to indicate children who are between levels. For example, children who create appropriate number stories but then illustrate them incorrectly might be identified as Beginning+.

Many teachers have found it helpful to compile children's number stories into books (either individual or whole class). Children may look these over in their free time or check them out to take home. Comparing the content of books made near the beginning of the year with those made at the end offers a clear picture of the progress children have made. Children may find it motivating when they see the progress they've made. Number stories from the beginning and the end of the year might make good portfolio entries.

Developing (D)

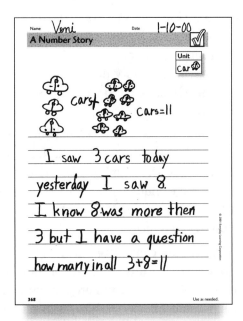

Secure (S)

Example 2: "What's My Rule?"

"What's My Rule?" routines involve problem solving, patterning, number sense and numeration, reasoning, and whole-number operations.

Time Frame: Use during or after Lessons 5.13 and 9.2.

"What's My Rule?" routines are introduced in Lesson 5.12. Initially, assess children's progress during Lesson 5.13 with journal page 127; Home Link 5.13; or Grade 1, Assessment Master B, which appears on *Math Masters* page 369. You may also do this assessment as a Math Box.

Do your second assessment after Lesson 9.2. Use journal page 210 or *Math Masters,* page 369.

Sample "What's My Rule?" Rubric

Sample Rubric

Beginning (B)
Children require much assistance. They are unable to complete all tables correctly, even with assistance.

Sample Rubric

Developing (D)
Children complete the "What's My Rule?" table but may require some assistance using larger numbers or creating another table. A few errors may be made, or the correct rule may not be given.

Sample Rubric

Secure (S)
Children correctly complete the "What's My Rule?" table, state the rule, and create their own table and rule with little or no assistance. The table is not limited to small numbers.

If you wish, use a plus symbol (+) to indicate children who are between levels. For example, a Developing+ child may show all of the signs of Secure children except for a few arithmetic errors.

Use the information from this assessment to help you plan instruction. If you have a number of children classified as Beginning, plan to work with them individually or in small groups. Alternatively, you may wish to include some "What's My Rule?" activities in Math Boxes or Math Messages. You may want to provide those children who are Secure with tables that include more difficult rules, larger numbers, or even negative numbers.

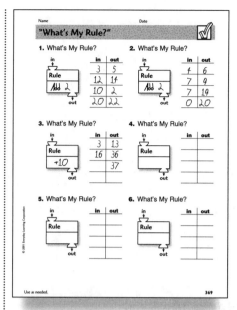

Beginning (B)

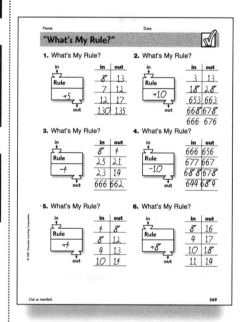

Secure (S)

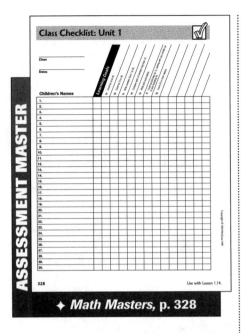

Math Masters, p. 328

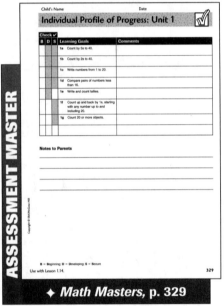

Math Masters, p. 329

NOTE: Class Checklists and Individual Profiles of Progress are only two parts of your assessment program. Observations of children as they work, as well as samples of their work, are necessary to provide a full picture of children's understandings and abilities.

Class Checklists and Individual Profiles of Progress

Class Checklists and Individual Profiles of Progress are provided for each unit as well as for each quarter. These checklists and profile masters list the learning goals identified for the end-of-unit oral and written assessments. They are found at the back of your *Math Masters* book and are in the Assessment Masters section of this book on pages 78–91.

First, use the Class Checklists to gather and record information. Then, transfer selected information to the Individual Profiles of Progress sheet for each child's portfolio or for use during parent conferences.

The information recorded on the checklists can be obtained from end-of-unit oral and written assessments. In fact, you may want to bypass the Class Checklists and record this information from these assessments directly onto the Individual Profiles of Progress.

Blank profile and checklist masters can be found on *Math Masters*, pages 355 and 356. You may wish to record information from other sources, such as journal review pages, Math Boxes, Math Messages, and Math Logs.

Information obtained from teacher-directed small groups and organized during Explorations, game time, or any other time is also a good resource to be recorded on the Class Checklists or directly on Individual Profiles of Progress. As mentioned in the Ongoing Assessment section of this book, information can be obtained from observations, questions, and other sources during regular instructional interactions as well.

When you use Class Checklists and Individual Profiles of Progress, consider using a rubric-recording method, such as Beginning, Developing, or Secure, to indicate progress. After children have had more experience and time with various concepts and skills, repeat needed assessment activities to assess progress further.

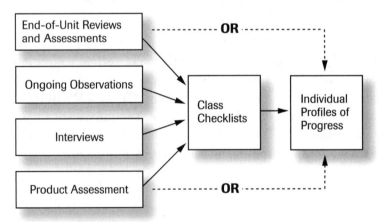

As an additional resource, you may choose to use *Math Masters*, page 357, which provides additional blank "Names" columns if you need to change the order for listing children's names on your master Class Checklist.

Individual Mathematical Interviews

Periodically interview children individually over the course of the year. These interviews should be kept short (10 to 15 minutes long at most). Getting to each child is not something that can be done very often, but even a couple of times a year should suffice.

Main objectives of interviews

- To show children that you are concerned about them as individuals
- To get to know children better
- To find out how children feel about mathematics and what they know about it

When to hold interviews

Interviews can be conducted while the rest of the class is playing games or during fairly independent Explorations. Teachers have also suggested that, if feasible, you can make "appointments" to have lunch with children individually or with two or three children at a time. Other appointments might be scheduled before class begins, during recess, or after school.

Suggestions for starting interviews

The focus of these interviews should reflect the information you are interested in discovering from individual children. Sample questions you may want to ask are:

- *How do you feel about mathematics?*
- *What have you enjoyed most about mathematics this year?*
- *What has been the easiest part of mathematics for you?*
- *What has been the hardest part of mathematics for you?*
- *How can we work together to help you feel more comfortable with these difficult parts of mathematics?*
- *How do you feel about working with partners and in small groups for some mathematics activities?*
- *How do you feel about Home Links? About Math Boxes?*

Children's responses might be taped or recorded on an individual interview sheet.

Math Interest Inventories

At the beginning of the year, you may want children to complete an inventory to assess their mathematical attitudes. This inventory might be repeated later in the year to see if their attitudes have changed. A grade-level sample (About My Math Class) is given in *Math Masters,* page 361. Inventories can be included in children's portfolios and discussed during individual interviews or parent conferences. For younger children, discussion of portfolios might be best done in individual or small-group interviews.

Parent Reflections

Parents can also be included in the assessment process. Prior to conferences, you can send parents a Parent Reflections page. A sample is given below. A blank Parent Reflections form is provided on *Math Masters,* page 359. The prompts are designed to focus parents' concerns prior to conferences.

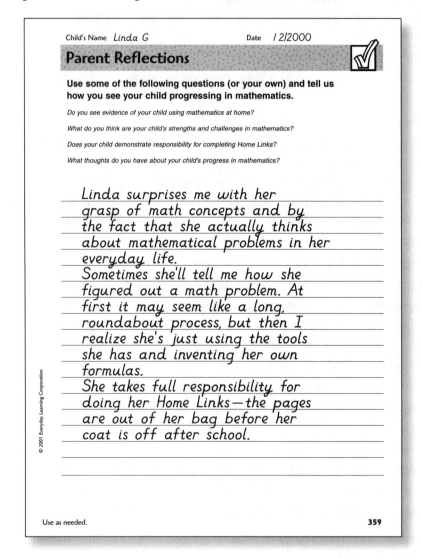

Child's Name Linda G   Date 1/2/2000

Parent Reflections

Use some of the following questions (or your own) and tell us how you see your child progressing in mathematics.

Do you see evidence of your child using mathematics at home?

What do you think are your child's strengths and challenges in mathematics?

Does your child demonstrate responsibility for completing Home Links?

What thoughts do you have about your child's progress in mathematics?

Linda surprises me with her grasp of math concepts and by the fact that she actually thinks about mathematical problems in her everyday life.

Sometimes she'll tell me how she figured out a math problem. At first it may seem like a long, roundabout process, but then I realize she's just using the tools she has and inventing her own formulas.

She takes full responsibility for doing her Home Links—the pages are out of her bag before her coat is off after school.

Use as needed.   359

Outside Tests

Many teachers are responsible for outside tests or assessments that are mandated by their schools, districts, or states. These tests vary widely, from traditional standardized tests with multiple-choice responses to more performance-based assessments. Because of the attention that is sometimes given to outside tests and assessments, many teachers worry whether *Everyday Mathematics* adequately prepares students, especially for the traditional standardized test formats.

Reports from teachers and school administrators indicate that *Everyday Mathematics* children generally do about as well on the computation sections of standardized tests—and much better on the concepts and problem-solving sections as students in traditional programs. Our research supports these anecdotal reports. However, traditional standardized tests do not assess the depth and breadth of the mathematical knowledge that should be attained by *Everyday Mathematics* children.

Many testing companies, as well as several states, districts, and schools, have recently developed performance assessments or open-ended tests. These tests indicate results similar to those from traditional tests—class and individual norms (percentile rankings)—but they also attempt to test problem-solving and communication skills on larger tasks. Some of these assessments provide rubric scores along with normed data.

Some standardized tests, along with many state tests, now allow the use of calculators on problem-solving sections because many students have access to them during instruction. Here are some further suggestions for handling outside tests:

• Rather than taking class time to "teach to the test," you may want to rely on Math Boxes and a systematic review of completed Math Boxes problems to help prepare children for the format of an outside test. It is our experience that it is the unfamiliar format and the test-taking conditions that disturb children, especially younger children, the most when taking outside tests.

NOTE: There are blank Math Boxes masters in the Teaching Aid Masters section of your *Math Masters* book (pages 141 and 142). You might want to use these to fill in your own Math Boxes problems.

- If your district test is based on traditional goals, work toward having it rewritten to match the National Council of Teachers of Mathematics *Assessment Standards* and the *Everyday Mathematics* curriculum.
- Encourage or consider the use of one of the newer performance-based tests in place of the traditional multiple-choice standardized tests. As much as possible, outside tests should reflect the instructional practices of the classroom.

Your Assessment Ideas

_____

_____

_____

_____

_____

_____

_____

_____

_____

_____

_____

_____

_____

_____

_____

_____

_____

_____

_____

_____

_____

_____

Recommended Reading

Black, Paul, and Dylan Wiliam. "Assessment and Classroom Learning." *Assessment in Education* (March, 1998): 7–74.

——. "Inside the Black Box: Raising Standards Through Classroom Assessment." *Phi Delta Kappan* 80, no. 2 (October, 1998): 139–149.

Bryant, Brian R., and Teddy Maddox. "Using Alternative Assessment Techniques to Plan and Evaluate Mathematics." *LD Forum* 21, no. 2 (winter, 1996): 24–33.

Eisner, Elliot W. "The Uses and Limits of Performance Assessment." *Phi Delta Kappan* 80, no. 9 (May, 1999): 658–661.

Kuhn, Gerald. *Mathematics Assessment: What Works in the Classroom.* San Francisco: Jossey-Bass Publishers, 1994.

National Council of Teachers of Mathematics (NCTM). *Curriculum and Evaluation Standards for School Mathematics.* Reston, Va.: NCTM, 1989.

——. *Assessment Standards for School Mathematics.* Reston, Va.: NCTM, 1995.

——. *Principles and Standards for School Mathematics: Discussion Draft.* Prepared by the Standards 2000 Writing Group. Reston, Va.: NCTM, 1998.

National Research Council, Mathematical Sciences Education Board. *Measuring What Counts: A Conceptual Guide for Mathematics Assessment.* Washington, D.C.: National Academy Press, 1993.

Pearson, Bethyl, and Cathy Berghoff. "London Bridge Is Not Falling Down: It's Supporting Alternative Assessment." *TESOL* Journal 5, no. 4 (summer, 1996): 28–31.

Shepard, Lorrie A. "Using Assessment to Improve Learning." *Educational Leadership* 52, no. 5 (February, 1995): 38–43.

Stenmark, Jean Kerr, ed. *Mathematics Assessment: Myths, Models, Good Questions, and Practical Suggestions.* Reston, Va.: National Council of Teachers of Mathematics, 1991.

Stiggens, Richard J. *Student-Centered Classroom Assessment.* Englewood Cliffs, N.J.: Prentice-Hall, 1997.

Webb, N. L., and A. F. Coxford, eds. *Assessment in the Mathematics Classroom: 1993 Yearbook.* Reston, Va.: National Council of Teachers of Mathematics, 1993.

Your Assessment Ideas

Assessment Overviews

This section offers examples for each unit of how to use different types of assessments in specific lessons. For each unit, you will find examples of three major types of assessment opportunities: Ongoing Assessment, Product Assessment, and Periodic Assessment. Keep in mind, however, that these are not distinct categories; they frequently overlap. For example, some Periodic Assessments also may serve as Product Assessments that you or the child may choose to keep in the child's portfolio.

Note: Unit 10 reviews previous units, so assessment examples for that unit are not included here.

Unit 1
Assessment Overview

There are many pathways to a balanced assessment plan. As you teach Unit 1, start to become familiar with some of the approaches to assessment. The next few pages offer examples of the three major types of assessment suggested in this program: Ongoing Assessment, Product Assessment, and Periodic Assessment. This assessment overview offers examples of ways to assess children on what they learn in Unit 1. Do not try to use all of the examples, but begin with a few that meet your needs.

Ongoing Assessment Opportunities

Ongoing assessment opportunities are opportunities to observe children during regular interactions, as they work independently and in groups. You can conduct ongoing assessment during teacher-guided instruction, Math Boxes sessions, mathematical mini-interviews, games, Mental Math and Reflexes sessions, strategy sharing, and slate work. The chart below provides a summary of ongoing assessment opportunities in Unit 1, as they relate to specific Unit 1 learning goals.

1d **Developing/Secure Goal** Compare pairs of numbers less than 16. (Lessons 1.2–1.4, 1.6, 1.7, and 1.10)	Lesson 1.6, p. 36
1e **Developing Goal** Write and count tallies. (Lessons 1.2, 1.7, 1.8, and 1.12)	Lesson 1.8, p. 44
1f **Secure Goal** Count up and back by 1s, starting with any number up to and including 20. (Lessons 1.1–1.5,1.7, and 1.9–1.11)	Lesson 1.5, p. 32 Lesson 1.6, p. 36
1g **Secure Goal** Count 20 or more objects. (Lessons 1.1–1.5, 1.8, 1.10, and 1.13)	Lesson 1.13, p. 69

Product Assessment Opportunities

Math Journals, Math Boxes, activity sheets, masters, Math Logs, and the results of Explorations and Projects all provide product assessment opportunities. On the next page is an example of how you might use a rubric to assess children's ability to write numbers.

Number Writing Lesson 1.13, p. 70; *Math Masters,* p. 2

Collect the pages on which children have written their numbers after they have circled their best efforts. The sample rubric below can help you evaluate children's work.

Portfolio Ideas

Sample Rubric
Beginning (B) The child attempts to write each number but does not exhibit correct formation. Many numbers are above and below the solid lines and are sometimes difficult to read. The number formations may also take up half or less of the space, instead of the entire space provided. The child may not begin his or her formation of the number at the correct location and may have his or her own process for trying to form the number. The child does not follow the arrows given on the page as reminders of the strokes for efficient number writing. Reversal of numbers may be present.
Developing (D) The child attempts to write each number. Formation of the numbers is progressing. The child is starting to utilize all of the space provided. The child may still have difficulty staying on the lines and sometimes needs to be reminded about where to begin and end the formation of the number. Reversal of numbers may still be present.
Secure (S) The child forms each number correctly. Each number is made using the entire line, and the numbers begin and end at the appropriate location. The child writes on the lines, and number reversals are not present. The child has correct formation of all of the numbers 1 through 6.

Periodic Assessment Opportunities

Here is a summary of the periodic assessment opportunities that are provided in Unit 1. Refer to Lesson 1.14 for details.

Oral and Slate Assessment

In Lesson 1.14, you will find oral and slate assessment problems on pages 72 and 73.

Written Assessment

In Lesson 1.14, you will find written assessment problems on page 74 (*Math Masters,* page 303).

See the chart below and on the next page to find oral, slate, and written assessment problems that address specific learning goals.

> NOTE: This sample rubric can be utilized in Unit 2, as children will continue to write the numbers 7, 8, 9, and 0. *Math Masters,* page 2 can be used as often as necessary to assess children in writing numbers.

1a **Developing/Secure Goal** Count by 5s to 40. (Lessons 1.4, 1.7, and 1.11)	Oral Assessment, Problem 3
1b **Developing/Secure Goal** Count by 2s to 40. (Lessons 1.9–1.13)	Oral Assessment, Problem 4
1c **Developing/Secure Goal** Write numbers from 1 to 20. (Lessons 1.4, 1.5, and 1.7–1.11)	Slate Assessment, Problems 1–7 Written Assessment, Problems 1, 3, and 6
1d **Developing/Secure Goal** Compare pairs of numbers less than 16. (Lessons 1.2–1.4, 1.6, 1.7, and 1.10)	Slate Assessment, Problems 1–5 Written Assessment, Problems 3–5

1e **Developing Goal** Write and count tallies. (Lessons 1.2, 1.7, 1.8, and 1.12)	Written Assessment, Problems 1 and 2
1f **Secure Goal** Count up and back by 1s, starting with any number up to and including 20. (Lessons 1.1–1.5, 1.7, and 1.9–1.11)	Oral Assessment, Problems 1 and 2 Written Assessment, Problem 3
1g **Secure Goal** Count 20 or more objects. (Lessons 1.1–1.5, 1.8, 1.10, and 1.13)	Slate Assessment, Problems 6 and 7 Written Assessment, Problem 3

Alternative Assessment

In Lesson 1.14, you will find alternative assessment options on pages 74 and 75.

✦ Bundle Craft Sticks

Use this activity from Lesson 1.4 to assess children's skill in counting objects (rational counting). Record your observations on Flip Cards (see page 13) or a Class Checklist (see page 14).

As you observe children, consider the following:

• Are they making a one-to-one correspondence between craft stick and number?

• Are they able to make a connection between the number of craft sticks counted and the number itself?

✦ Play *Top-It*

Use this game to assess children's skill in comparing numbers. Collect papers and save them for children's portfolios. This activity can be repeated later in the year to assess growth in writing and comparing numbers. Record your observations on Flip Cards (see page 13) or a Class Checklist (see page 14).

✦ Play *Number-Line Squeeze*

Use this game to assess children's skill in comparing and ordering numbers. Record observations on Flip Cards (see page 13). Consider the following when making observations during the game:

• Is the child able to move the brackets correctly based on the answer to his or her question? For example, "My number is greater than that."

• Does the child answering the questions give correct responses? For example, you ask a child with the number 8, "Is your number 10?" The child says, "No, my number is less than that."

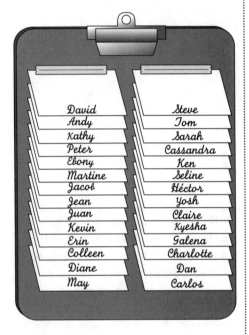

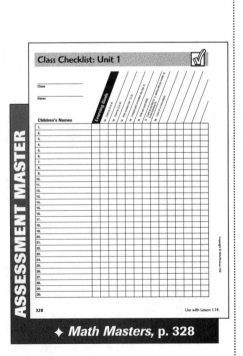

✦ Math Masters, p. 328

Unit 2
Assessment Overview

If you tried some of the assessment approaches that were suggested in the Unit 1 Assessment Overview, you are probably beginning to appreciate how the goal charts in this section can help you plan your assessment strategies. For example, the chart below alerts you to the fact that ongoing assessment opportunities related to Goal 2a are provided in Lesson 2.10 on page 132 of your *Teacher's Lesson Guide*. In similar fashion, you can use the chart on page 40 to find a written assessment opportunity related to this same goal.

Ongoing Assessment Opportunities

Ongoing assessment opportunities are opportunities to observe children during regular interactions, as they work independently and in groups. You can conduct ongoing assessment during teacher-guided instruction, Math Boxes sessions, mathematical mini-interviews, games, Mental Math and Reflexes sessions, strategy sharing, and slate work. The chart below provides a summary of ongoing assessment opportunities in Unit 2, as they relate to specific Unit 2 learning goals.

2a	**Developing/Secure Goal** Calculate the values of combinations of pennies and nickels. (Lessons 2.10–2.13)	Lesson 2.10, p. 132
2b	**Developing Goal** Find complements of 10. (Lessons 2.3, 2.10, and 2.12)	Lesson 2.3, p. 98
2d	**Developing/Secure Goal** Count up and back by 1s on the number grid. (Lessons 2.1–2.4)	Lesson 2.1, p. 90
2e	**Developing/Secure Goal** Tell time to the nearest hour. (Lessons 2.5, 2.6, and 2.13)	Lesson 2.5, p. 109 Lesson 2.6, p. 114
2f	**Developing/Secure Goal** Exchange pennies for nickels. (Lessons 2.9–2.11 and 2.13)	Lesson 2.9, p. 128 Lesson 2.10, p. 132

Product Assessment Opportunities

Math Journals, Math Boxes, activity sheets, masters, Math Logs, and the results of Explorations and Projects all provide product assessment opportunities. On the next page is an example of how you might use a rubric to assess children's knowledge of simple addition facts for sums of 10.

Lesson 2.14, p. 152

ALTERNATIVE ASSESSMENT **Find 2-Addend Combinations for Sums of 10**

Use this activity from Lesson 2.4 to assess how children are progressing with simple addition facts for sums of 10. The sample rubric below can help you evaluate children's progress in generating the combinations for the sums of 10.

Portfolio Ideas

Sample Rubric
Beginning (B) The child attempts to generate a list of the combinations for sums of 10 but may require some teacher assistance. The child is able to produce only one to four different solutions. The list may not be organized, but random (such as 0 + 10, 5 + 5, 8 + 2).
Developing (D) The child is able to get started generating a list of combinations without teacher assistance. The child generates five to nine possibilities. The child attempts to organize the list. Some children may have only six combinations listed (0 + 10, 1 + 9, 2 + 8, 3 + 7, 4 + 6, and 5 + 5), neglecting to include turn-around facts.
Secure (S) The child is able to generate all 11 possibilities (but may leave one out). The child organizes the list. The child understands not only the six combinations, but also the turn-around facts for each (0 + 10, 1 + 9, 2 + 8, 3 + 7, 4 + 6, 5 + 5, 6 + 4, 7 + 3, 8 + 2, 9 + 1, 10 + 0).

Periodic Assessment Opportunities

Here is a summary of the periodic assessment opportunities that are provided in Unit 2. Refer to Lesson 2.14 for details.

Oral and Slate Assessment

In Lesson 2.14, you will find oral and slate assessment problems on pages 150 and 151.

Written Assessment

In Lesson 2.14, you will find written assessment problems on page 151 (*Math Masters*, page 304).

See the chart below and on the next page to find oral, slate, and written assessment problems that address specific learning goals.

2a **Developing/Secure Goal** Calculate the values of combinations of pennies and nickels. (Lessons 2.10–2.13)	Written Assessment, Problems 3–5
2b **Developing Goal** Find complements of 10. (Lessons 2.3, 2.10, and 2.12)	Slate Assessment, Problem 6
2c **Developing Goal** Solve addition and subtraction number stories. (Lessons 2.6–2.8, 2.10, 2.12, and 2.13)	Slate Assessment, Problems 3 and 6
2d **Developing/Secure Goal** Count up and back by 1s on the number grid. (Lessons 2.1–2.4)	Oral Assessment, Problem 5 Slate Assessment, Problem 1

2e	**Developing/Secure Goal** Tell time to the nearest hour. (Lessons 2.5, 2.6, and 2.13)	Oral Assessment, Problem 6 Written Assessment, Problems 1 and 2
2f	**Developing/Secure Goal** Exchange pennies for nickels. (Lessons 2.9–2.11 and 2.13)	Written Assessment, Problem 5
2g	**Secure Goal** Count by 2s to 40. Count by 5s to 50. (Lessons 2.2, 2.4, 2.7, 2.9, 2.10, and 2.13)	Oral Assessment, Problems 1–3

Alternative Assessment

In Lesson 2.14, you will find alternative assessment options on page 152.

✦ **Play** *Two-Fisted Penny Addition*

Use this game from Lesson 2.3 to assess children's understanding of sums of 10, as well as their skill in counting objects (rational counting). Record your observations using Flip Cards (see page 13) or a Class Checklist (see page 14).

Which types of strategies are children using to arrive at the solution?

• Do they count on the needed number to make 10?

• Are they starting over from 1 each time to make 10?

• Do some children always come up with a number that adds up to more than 10?

• Do some children still rely on *Math Masters,* page 9 as an organizational tool?

✦ **Find 2-Addend Combinations for Sums of 10**

Use this activity from Lesson 2.4 to assess how children are progressing with simple addition facts for sums of 10. Use the sample rubric given under Product Assessment Opportunities to help evaluate children's progress.

✦ **Play** *Nickel/Penny Grab*

Use this game to assess children's understanding of counting nickels and pennies. Record your observations on the Class Checklist (see page 14).

• Do children exchange five pennies for a nickel?

• Are they able to count their coins by counting by 5s with the nickels and then adding on the pennies? Or do children want to start over in the counting when adding on the pennies?

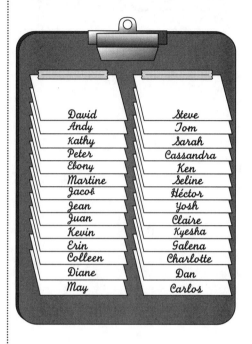

✦ *Math Masters,* p. 330

Unit 3
Assessment Overview

In this unit, children are asked to complete Frames-and-Arrows diagrams (see Goal 3a in the chart below). The Frames-and-Arrows routine will be used throughout first grade and will extend into second and third grades to incorporate more than one rule and to use a variety of concepts. Children's progress with this routine can be tracked using portfolio assessment. Suggestions for assessing children's work products, using a rubric, are provided on page 43.

Ongoing Assessment Opportunities

Ongoing assessment opportunities are opportunities to observe children during regular interactions, as they work independently and in groups. You can conduct ongoing assessment during teacher-guided instruction, Math Boxes sessions, mathematical mini-interviews, games, Mental Math and Reflexes sessions, strategy sharing, and slate work. The chart below provides a summary of ongoing assessment opportunities in Unit 3, as they relate to specific Unit 3 learning goals.

3a	**Beginning/Developing Goal** Complete Frames-and-Arrows diagrams. (Lessons 3.8, 3.9, and 3.11)	Lesson 3.8, p. 204
3b	**Developing Goal** Identify and complete patterns. (Lessons 3.1–3.5, 3.13, and 3.14)	Lesson 3.1, p. 169
3c	**Developing Goal** Solve addition and subtraction problems by skip counting on the number line and the number grid. (Lessons 3.3–3.7 and 3.9)	Lesson 3.5, p. 190 Lesson 3.6, p. 194
3d	**Developing Goal** Identify numbers as even or odd. (Lessons 3.2–3.5, 3.13, and 3.14)	Lesson 3.2, p. 175
3e	**Developing Goal** Know the values of pennies, nickels, and dimes, and calculate the values of combinations of these coins. (Lessons 3.2, 3.4, and 3.10–3.13)	Lesson 3.11, p. 221 Lesson 3.12, p. 225
3f	**Developing Goal** Tell time to the nearest half-hour. (Lessons 3.5, 3.7, and 3.8)	Lesson 3.7, p. 198
3g	**Developing Goal** Solve addition and subtraction number stories. (Lessons 3.6 and 3.11–3.13)	Lesson 3.6, p. 194

Product Assessment Opportunities

Math Journals, Math Boxes, activity sheets, masters, Math Logs, and the results of Explorations and Projects all provide product assessment opportunities. Here are some ideas for assessing children's work products in Unit 3.

For each of the following activities, give children Frames-and-Arrows problems based on their needs. The sample rubric below can help you evaluate children's progress. You can use *Math Masters,* page 28 for any of the activities indicated.

Lesson 3.8, p. 205
EXTRA PRACTICE **Solving Frames-and-Arrows Problems**

Lesson 3.9, p. 208
Making up Frames-and-Arrows Problems

Lesson 3.15, p. 240
ALTERNATIVE ASSESSMENT **Complete Frames- and-Arrows Diagrams**

Portfolio Ideas

Sample Rubric

Beginning (B)
The child has difficulty getting started and needs assistance from the teacher. The child is given the rule, and at least the first frame is filled in. The child is unable to complete all the frames completely. Operational errors are made.

Developing (D)
The child can complete Frames-and-Arrows problems given the rule and at least the first frame with little assistance or error. However, the child has difficulty generating the rule from a Frames-and-Arrows diagram. The child is able to make up his or her own Frames-and-Arrows problems that consist of a rule and at least the first frame.

Secure (S)
The child can complete Frames-and-Arrows problems that have the first frame (or first few frames) missing by working backwards or thinking about the inverse operation. The child is also able to make his or her own Frames-and-Arrows problems, leaving the first frames blank and giving the rule.

Periodic Assessment Opportunities

Here is a summary of the periodic assessment opportunities that are provided in Unit 3. Refer to Lesson 3.15 for details.

Oral and Slate Assessment

In Lesson 3.15, you will find oral and slate assessment problems on pages 237 and 238.

Written Assessment

In Lesson 3.15, you will find written assessment problems on page 239 (*Math Masters,* pages 305 and 306).

See the chart below to find oral, slate, and written assessment problems that address specific learning goals.

3a **Beginning/Developing Goal** Complete Frames-and-Arrows diagrams. (Lessons 3.8, 3.9, and 3.11)	Written Assessment, Problem 4
3b **Developing Goal** Identify and complete patterns. (Lessons 3.1–3.5, 3.13, and 3.14)	Written Assessment, Problem 4
3c **Developing Goal** Solve addition and subtraction problems by skip counting on the number line and the number grid. (Lessons 3.3–3.7 and 3.9)	Oral Assessment, Problems 1, 2, and 3 Slate Assessment, Problem 1 Written Assessment, Problem 5
3d **Developing Goal** Identify numbers as even or odd. (Lessons 3.2–3.5, 3.13, and 3.14)	Slate Assessment, Problem 5 Written Assessment, Problem 2
3e **Developing Goal** Know the values of pennies, nickels, and dimes, and calculate the values of combinations of these coins. (Lessons 3.2, 3.4, and 3.10–3.13)	Written Assessment, Problem 3
3f **Developing Goal** Tell time to the nearest half-hour. (Lessons 3.5, 3.7, and 3.8)	Oral Assessment, Problem 4 Written Assessment, Problem 1
3g **Developing Goal** Solve addition and subtraction number stories. (Lessons 3.6 and 3.11–3.13)	Slate Assessment, Problem 3

Alternative Assessment

In Lesson 3.15, you will find alternative assessment options on pages 239 and 240.

✦ Identify and Complete Patterns

To assess understanding of identifying and extending patterns, have children make a pattern with various objects, such as pattern blocks, craft sticks, or attribute blocks. Record your observations on Flip Cards (see page 13) or a Class Checklist (see page 14).

Make some of the following observations:

• Are children able to create patterns that can be extended?
• Are the patterns easy or complex? (ABAB, AABBCC, ABCABC)
• Do children create a variety of patterns, or do they rely on the same pattern each time?
• Are children able to extend patterns when given the first part?

✦ Play *Coin-Dice*

To evaluate their ability to make exchanges among pennies, nickels, and dimes, have pairs of children play this game. This game will also help you to evaluate children's ability to count collections of coins. Record observations on Flip Cards (see page 13).

Keep the following in mind when making observations:

- Are some children not ready to make exchanges with dimes? Are they still developing their skills with penny and nickel exchanges?
- Do children see the many different ways to make exchanges for a dime—5 pennies and 1 nickel, 2 nickels, 10 pennies?
- Are children able to keep a running total of the value of the coins collected?

✦ **Complete Frames-and-Arrows Diagrams**

See *Math Masters,* page 28. Also refer to the suggestions and the sample rubric under Product Assessment Opportunities.

Portfolio Ideas

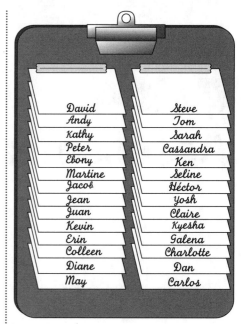

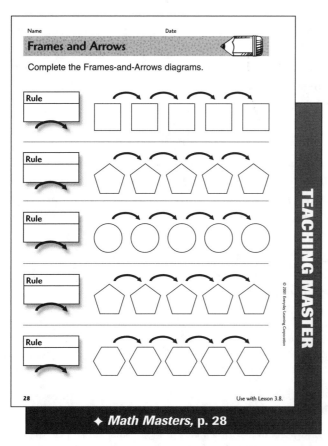

✦ *Math Masters, p. 28*

✦ **Order Clocks**

Use this activity to assess how well children understand time. Children set their tool-kit clocks to a specified time given by the teacher. This activity also evaluates understanding of ordering the clocks from the earliest time to the latest time. Have children work in small groups to complete this task. Use Flip Cards to record your observations. Assess whether children display the correct time and then note which children understand how to put the clocks in order from earliest time to latest.

✦ *Math Masters, p. 332*

Unit 4
Assessment Overview

At this point in the *Everyday Mathematics* program, you might consider whether you are beginning to establish a balance of Ongoing, Product, and Periodic Assessment strategies. Also, think about whether your strategies include both keeping anecdotal records based on observations of children's progress and using written assessments.

Ongoing Assessment Opportunities

Ongoing assessment opportunities are opportunities to observe children during regular interactions, as they work independently and in groups. You can conduct ongoing assessment during teacher-guided instruction, Math Boxes sessions, mathematical mini-interviews, games, Mental Math and Reflexes sessions, strategy sharing, and slate work. The chart below provides a summary of ongoing assessment opportunities in Unit 4, as they relate to specific Unit 4 learning goals.

4a	**Developing Goal** Use standard units for measuring length. (Lessons 4.3–4.7)	Lesson 4.3, p. 267 Lesson 4.4, p. 272 Lesson 4.5, p. 278 Lesson 4.6, p. 283
4b	**Developing Goal** Find sums and missing addends. (Lessons 4.1, 4.2, 4.5–4.9, 4.11, and 4.12)	Lesson 4.11, p. 311 Lesson 4.12, p. 314
4f	**Developing/Secure Goal** Tell time to the nearest half-hour. (Lessons 4.4, 4.5, 4.8, and 4.9)	Lesson 4.8, p. 294

Product Assessment Opportunities

Math Journals, Math Boxes, activity sheets, masters, Math Logs, and the results of Explorations and Projects all provide product assessment opportunities. On the next page is an example of how you might use a rubric to assess children's understanding of parts and totals by drawing numbers in a blank domino.

Lesson 4.11, p. 308
Math Message Follow-Up

Collect the half-sheets of paper that contain children's drawings of dominoes and the numbers that go with them. The sample rubric below can help you evaluate children's work.

Portfolio Ideas

Sample Rubric
Beginning (B) The child attempts to draw a domino but either leaves it blank or has difficulty drawing in the correct number of dots without assistance.
Developing (D) The child is able to correctly add dots to the domino but requires assistance to total them.
Secure (S) The child is able to draw a domino on his or her own and then correctly add dots to the domino and total them.

Periodic Assessment Opportunities

Here is a summary of the periodic assessment opportunities that are provided in Unit 4. Refer to Lesson 4.13 for details.

Oral and Slate Assessment

In Lesson 4.13, you will find oral and slate assessment problems on pages 318–320.

Written Assessment

In Lesson 4.13, you will find written assessment problems on page 320 (*Math Masters,* pages 307 and 308).

See the chart below to find oral, slate, and written assessment problems that address specific learning goals.

4a **Developing Goal** Use standard units for measuring length. (Lessons 4.3–4.7)	Written Assessment, Problems 3–6
4b **Developing Goal** Find sums and missing addends. (Lessons 4.1, 4.2, 4.5–4.9, 4.11, and 4.12)	Written Assessment, Problems 8–13
4c **Developing Goal** Calculate the values of combinations of pennies, nickels, and dimes. (Lessons 4.3 and 4.10)	Written Assessment, Problem 7 Slate Assessment, Problem 2
4d **Developing Goal** Solve addition and subtraction number stories. (Lessons 4.3, 4.6, 4.7, and 4.9)	Slate Assessment, Problem 9
4e **Developing/Secure Goal** Order and compare numbers to 22. (Lessons 4.1, 4.5, 4.8, 4.11, and 4.12)	Slate Assessment, Problems 3 and 4
4f **Developing/Secure Goal** Tell time to the nearest half-hour. (Lessons 4.4, 4.5, 4.8, and 4.9)	Written Assessment, Problem 1 Oral Assessment, Problem 5

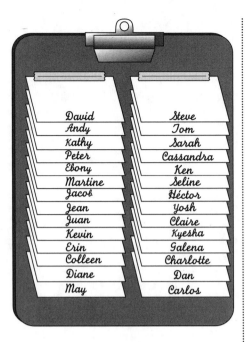

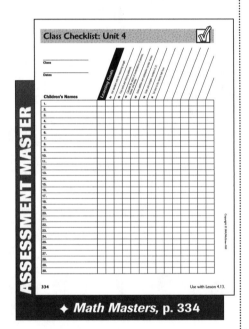

Class Checklist: Unit 4

Class

Dates

Children's Names

334　Use with Lesson 4.13.

✦ *Math Masters, p. 334*

Alternative Assessment

In Lesson 4.13, you will find alternative assessment options on pages 320 and 321.

✦ **Play *Domino Top-It***

Even though children will turn in half-sheets of paper with their domino drawings and dot totals, you might also choose to circulate as they play *Domino Top-It* and use Flip Cards or a Class Checklist to record their progress. Alternatively, you can use a rubric similar to the one you used at the beginning of this lesson to evaluate children's written work. Concentrate on the following:

• Did children write the correct total number of dots for the domino?

• Ask each child whether his or her total number of dots is larger or smaller than the total on his or her partner's domino.

✦ **Make a Measurement Page**

Use the activity *Making a Measurement Book* from Lesson 4.6 to assess children's ability to measure and record the lengths of a variety of objects. Keep questions like the following in mind as you circulate:

• Have children measured each object correctly?

• Did children measure to the nearest quarter-inch, half-inch, or inch?

• Did children include objects longer than their 6-inch rulers? If so, were they able to measure these objects?

✦ **Order Clocks**

Use the activity *Ordering Clocks by the Time They Display* from Lesson 4.8 to assess children's ability to order clocks set to different times. As you circulate, watch for the following:

• Can children determine the difference between a clock set on the quarter-hour and a clock set on the half-hour?

• Is it readily apparent to children which is later: a time shown as a quarter past the hour or a time shown as three-quarters past the same hour?

Unit 5
Assessment Overview

In this unit, children are introduced to the "What's My Rule?" routine. Routines are used throughout *Everyday Mathematics* to help children master basic skills. The "What's My Rule?" routine provides a format for thinking about rule-based relationships between pairs of numbers. Goal 5a in the chart below and on page 50 suggests early assessment options for this routine. Background information on other routines is provided in the Management Guide section of the *Teacher's Reference Manual.*

Ongoing Assessment Opportunities

Ongoing assessment opportunities are opportunities to observe children during regular interactions, as they work alone and in groups. You can conduct ongoing assessment during teacher-guided instruction, Math Boxes, mathematical mini-interviews, games, Mental Math and Reflexes, strategy sharing, and slate work. The chart below provides a summary of ongoing assessment opportunities in Unit 5, as they relate to specific Unit 5 learning goals.

5a **Beginning/Developing Goal** Find missing numbers and/or the missing rule in "What's My Rule?" problems. (Lessons 5.10, 5.12, and 5.13)	Lesson 5.12, p. 391 Lesson 5.13, p. 395
5b **Developing Goal** Understand place value for tens and ones. (Lessons 5.1–5.5, 5.8, 5.9, 5.12, and 5.13)	Lesson 5.1, p. 336 Lesson 5.5, p. 357
5c **Developing Goal** Compare numbers using < and >. (Lessons 5.3, 5.6–5.9, 5.12, and 5.13)	Lesson 5.6, p. 362
5d **Developing Goal** Know +1, +0, doubles, and sums of 10 addition facts. (Lessons 5.4, 5.5, 5.7, and 5.9–5.11)	Lesson 5.9, p. 375
5e **Developing Goal** Solve addition and subtraction number stories. (Lessons 5.6–5.11)	Lesson 5.7, p. 367

Product Assessment Opportunities

Math Journals, Math Boxes, activity sheets, masters, Math Logs, and the results of Explorations and Projects all provide product assessment opportunities. On the next page is an example of how you might use a rubric to assess children's ability to write or illustrate a number story.

Lesson 5.8, p. 373

ENRICHMENT **Making A Classroom Number–Story Book**

Circulate around the room as children work in pairs to tell and write number stories. The sample rubric below can help you evaluate children's work.

Portfolio Ideas

Sample Rubric
Beginning (B)
The child attempts to write or illustrate a number story, but the story is incomplete and not connected to numbers. The child requires assistance throughout the process and no number model is present.
Developing (D)
The child is able to write or illustrate a number story with little assistance. No number model is present, or if there is a number model it does not match the number story.
Secure (S)
The child is able to write and/or illustrate a number story without assistance. The number story also has a correct number model to go along with it.

Periodic Assessment Opportunities

Here is a summary of the periodic assessment opportunities that are provided for Unit 5. Refer to Lesson 5.14 for details.

Oral and Slate Assessment

In Lesson 5.14, you will find oral and slate assessment problems on pages 399 and 400.

Written Assessment

In Lesson 5.14, you will find written assessment problems on page 400 (*Math Masters,* pages 309 and 310).

See the chart below to find oral, slate, and written assessment problems that address specific learning goals.

5a	**Beginning/Developing Goal** Find missing numbers and/or the missing rule in "What's My Rule?" problems. (Lessons 5.10, 5.12, and 5.13)	Written Assessment, Problems 16 and 17
5b	**Developing Goal** Understand place value for tens and ones. (Lessons 5.1–5.5, 5.8, 5.9, 5.12, and 5.13)	Oral Assessment, Problem 3 Slate Assessment, Problem 5 Written Assessment, Problems 9 and 10
5c	**Developing Goal** Compare numbers using $<$ and $>$. (Lessons 5.3–5.9, 5.12, and 5.13)	Written Assessment, Problems 11–14
5d	**Developing Goal** Know +1, +0, doubles, and sums of 10 addition facts. (Lessons 5.4, 5.5, 5.7, and 5.9–5.11)	Slate Assessment, Problem 4 Written Assessment, Problems 1–8
5e	**Developing Goal** Solve addition and subtraction number stories. (Lessons 5.6–5.11)	Slate Assessment, Problem 6 Written Assessment, Problem 15

Alternative Assessment

In Lesson 5.14, you will find alternative assessment options on page 401.

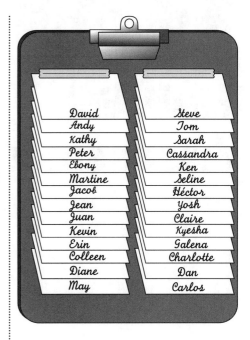

✦ **Play *Top-It* with Relation Symbols**

Circulate and assess children's ability to determine the correct symbol (<, >, or =) and to read the number model. Record your observation using Flip Cards or a Class Checklist. If necessary, remind children of the strategies for distinguishing between the two inequality symbols. For example, remind them that the "point" of the inequality symbol *points at* the smaller number.

Evaluate children's written results.

• Are they able to draw the inequality symbols correctly?

• Do they understand what the symbols mean?

• Are they able to consistently use the symbols correctly?

✦ **Play the *Tens-and-Ones Trading Game***

To evaluate whether or not children understand how to trade ten units for one long, ask children to record the results of each roll of the die. Then ask them to draw a picture, using units and longs, to show how they traded units for longs at each step along the way in order to build their total score using the fewest blocks. Look at children's drawings to ensure that they understand that ten ones make one ten. Ask them to explain their drawings to you.

✦ *Math Masters*, p. 336

Unit 6
Assessment Overview

Unit 6 focuses on developing fact power and reviews many of the skills introduced in earlier units. Fact power means that children need to develop the ability to recall basic addition facts instantly, without having to take time to figure them out. Games are an integral part of *Everyday Mathematics* and are used to reinforce children's memorization of basic facts. References to games are given in the Alternative Assessment sections of this book on pages 38, 41, 44, 48, 51, 54, and 60.

Ongoing Assessment Opportunities

Ongoing assessment opportunities are opportunities to observe children during regular interactions, as they work independently and in groups. You can conduct ongoing assessment during teacher-guided instruction, Math Boxes sessions, mathematical mini-interviews, games, Mental Math and Reflexes sessions, strategy sharing, and slate work. The chart below provides a summary of ongoing assessment opportunities in Unit 6, as they relate to specific Unit 6 learning goals.

6a **Beginning Goal** Measure objects to the nearest centimeter. (Lessons 6.6, 6.7, and 6.9)	Lesson 6.6, p. 515
6c **Beginning/Developing Goal** Know addition facts. (Lessons 6.1–6.5, 6.7, 6.11, and 6.12)	Lesson 6.1, p. 489
6d **Beginning/Developing Goal** Calculate the values of combinations of pennies, nickels, dimes, and quarters. (Lessons 6.8–6.10 and 6.12)	Lesson 6.9, p. 530
6e **Developing Goal** Find equivalent names for a number. (Lessons 6.2 and 6.3)	Lesson 6.2, p. 495

Product Assessment Opportunities

Math Journals, Math Boxes, activity sheets, masters, Math Logs, and the results of Explorations and Projects all provide product assessment opportunities. On the next page is an example of how you might use a rubric to assess children's understanding of the relationships among pattern blocks.

Lesson 6.7, p. 519

EXPLORATION A **Finding the Relationships among Pattern Blocks**

Children determine how many of one kind of a smaller pattern block are needed to cover a larger pattern block. Then they draw the arrangement of the smaller blocks on the larger block. The sample rubric below can help you evaluate children's work.

Sample Rubric
Beginning (B)
The child attempts to start the activity but requires much assistance. Once a shape has been covered with pattern blocks, the child also requires assistance in tracing the work.
Developing (D)
The child attempts the activity on his or her own. The child covers most of the larger pattern-block shapes correctly with only some assistance. The child also traces his or her work by using the template with little assistance.
Secure (S)
The child is able to cover the pattern-block shapes without assistance. The child also is able to transfer his or her work by using the template without assistance.

Periodic Assessment Opportunities

Here is a summary of the periodic assessment opportunities that are provided in Unit 6. Refer to Lesson 6.13 for details.

Oral and Slate Assessment

In Lesson 6.13, you will find oral and slate assessment problems on pages 550 and 551.

Written Assessment

In Lesson 6.13, you will find written assessment problems on page 552 (*Math Masters,* page 311).

See the chart below to find oral, slate, and written assessment problems that address specific learning goals.

6a	**Beginning Goal** Measure objects to the nearest centimeter. (Lessons 6.6, 6.7, and 6.9)	Written Assessment, Problems 3 and 4
6b	**Beginning Goal** Understand digital notation for time. (Lessons 6.10 and 6.11)	Slate Assessment, Problem 6 Written Assessment, Problems 1 and 2
6c	**Beginning/Developing Goal** Know addition facts. (Lessons 6.1–6.5, 6.7, 6.11, and 6.12)	Written Assessment, Problems 5–10
6d	**Beginning/Developing Goal** Calculate the values of combinations of pennies, nickels, dimes, and quarters. (Lessons 6.8–6.10 and 6.12)	Oral Assessment, Problem 5 Written Assessment, Problem 11
6e	**Developing Goal** Find equivalent names for a number. (Lessons 6.2 and 6.3)	Written Assessment, Problem 12

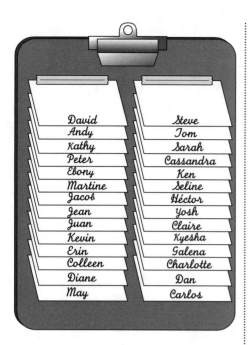

Alternative Assessment

In Lesson 6.13, you will find alternative assessment options on pages 552 and 553.

✦ Play *Beat the Calculator*

As children play this activity from Lesson 6.4 in groups of three, assess their ability to memorize addition facts. As you circulate, use a Class Checklist or Flip Cards to record children's progress. You can also have children record, on a half-sheet of paper, the facts for which they beat the calculator.

✦ Solve Name-Collection Box Problems

Use the activity *Introducing Name-Collection Boxes* from Lesson 6.2 to assess children's ability to find equivalent names for numbers. Collect the pages when children have finished and keep questions like the following in mind:

• Can children find a number of correct equivalent names for a number?

• Can children find ways other than adding to find equivalent names for numbers?

✦ Order Clocks

Assess children's progress in arranging clocks in the order of their times by using the cards from *Math Masters,* page 87 in Lesson 6.10. As they work in small groups, circulate and indicate children's progress on Class Checklists or Flip Cards. You also might collect children's written half-sheets of paper on which they have recorded the times in order. Keep the following questions in mind:

• Were children able to put the clocks in order?

• Did children have greater difficulty with quarter-hour times than with times that were on the hour or the half-hour?

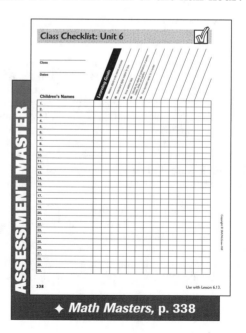

✦ *Math Masters,* p. 338

Unit 7
Assessment Overview

You may have noticed that all goals are assessed in some way in each unit. However, the method of assessment varies depending on the goal. For example, some goals are assessed more effectively using ongoing assessment, while others are better assessed using product or periodic assessment. In this unit, for example, as children are introduced to ideas about 3-dimensional shapes, three ongoing assessment opportunities are suggested that correspond to specific learning goals. All of the learning goals in the unit, however, can be assessed using oral, slate, or written assessments. This provides flexibility for you to choose those assessment opportunities that you find most appropriate for your classroom situation.

Ongoing Assessment Opportunities

Ongoing assessment opportunities are opportunities to observe children during regular interactions, as they work independently and in groups. You can conduct ongoing assessment during teacher-guided instruction, Math Boxes sessions, mathematical mini-interviews, games, Mental Math and Reflexes sessions, strategy sharing, and slate work. The chart below provides a summary of ongoing assessment opportunities in Unit 7, as they relate to specific Unit 7 learning goals.

7a **Beginning Goal** Identify 3-dimensional shapes and know their characteristics. (Lessons 7.5–7.7)	Lesson 7.6, p. 591
7c **Developing Goal** Sort and identify objects by attributes. (Lessons 7.1 and 7.2)	Lesson 7.1, p. 568
7d **Beginning/Developing Goal** Identify polygons and know their characteristics. (Lessons 7.3, 7.4, 7.6, and 7.7)	Lesson 7.4, p. 581

Product Assessment Opportunities

Math Journals, Math Boxes, activity sheets, masters, Math Logs, and the results of Explorations and Projects all provide product assessment opportunities. On the next page is an example of how you might use a rubric to assess children's ability to make attribute-block designs.

EXPLORATION B **Making Attribute-Block Designs**

Use this activity to assess children's ability to construct and color designs using attribute blocks. You may wish to create your own rubric, or use the sample rubric below to help you evaluate children's work.

Sample Rubric
Beginning (B) The child has difficulty making and copying the given designs and needs much assistance on both pages.
Developing (D) The child attempts to make and copy the given designs on his or her own. The second page might be more of a challenge and assistance may be needed.
Secure (S) The child makes and copies the designs on both pages without assistance. The child may also create other variations for the given designs.

Periodic Assessment Opportunities

Here is a summary of the periodic assessment opportunities that are provided in Unit 7. Refer to Lesson 7.8 for details.

Oral and Slate Assessment

In Lesson 7.8, you will find oral and slate assessment problems on pages 598 and 599.

Written Assessment

In Lesson 7.8, you will find written assessment problems on page 600 (*Math Masters,* pages 312 and 313).

See the chart below to find oral, slate, and written assessment problems that address specific learning goals.

7a	**Beginning Goal** Identify 3-dimensional shapes and know their characteristics. (Lessons 7.5–7.7)	Oral Assessment, Problem 4 Written Assessment, Problem 4
7b	**Beginning Goal** Identify symmetrical figures. (Lesson 7.7)	Written Assessment, Problem 3
7c	**Developing Goal** Sort and identify objects by attributes. (Lessons 7.1 and 7.2)	Oral Assessment, Problem 3 Written Assessment, Problem 2
7d	**Beginning/Developing Goal** Identify polygons and know their characteristics. (Lessons 7.3, 7.4, 7.6, and 7.7)	Oral Assessment, Problem 4 Written Assessment, Problem 1
7e	**Developing Goal** Know addition facts. (Lessons 7.2 and 7.6)	Slate Assessment, Problem 7 Written Assessment, Problem 5

Alternative Assessment

In Lesson 7.8, you will find alternative assessment options on pages 600 and 601.

✦ Draw a Picture with 2-Dimensional Shapes

In this activity, children are asked to draw a variety of 2-dimensional shapes and to outline each type of shape in a different color. To assess children's ability on these tasks, circulate and use a Class Checklist or Flip Cards to record progress. You might think about the following questions:

• How many shapes has each child drawn?

• Have children drawn and outlined shapes other than those asked for?

• Have children used different colors for each shape?

• Is there a shape that most children did not include?

✦ Match Shapes

In the activity *Matching Shape Attributes* from Lesson 7.5, children are asked to choose objects that match particular 3-dimensional shapes with respect to at least one characteristic. Circulate and assess children's ability, using Flip Cards or a Class Checklist. The following questions might be useful:

• Do children correctly identify common shape attributes?

• Can children choose a shape that is not the same as the one you have chosen but that has an attribute in common with it?

✦ Find Symmetry

In the activity *Making Symmetry Cards* from Lesson 7.7, children use mirrors to complete pictures on symmetry cards and create their own symmetry cards as well. To assess and record children's progress on identifying symmetrical objects, circulate and use Flip Cards or a Class Checklist. You might consider the following questions:

• Can children effectively use mirrors to create their symmetry cards?

• Can children correctly locate the axis of symmetry in making symmetry cards?

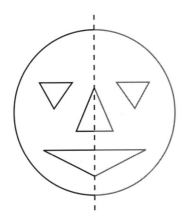

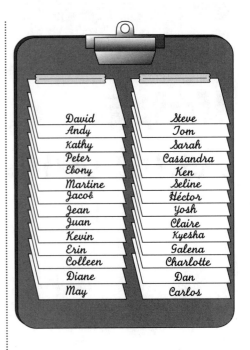

✦ *Math Masters*, p. 340

ASSESSMENT MASTER

Unit 8
Assessment Overview

In this unit, children further develop their ability to work with money and place value. Depending on the specific skill, children's ability levels might range from Beginning to Developing. A good mix of ongoing assessment opportunities for these skills is suggested in the chart below. Oral, written, and slate assessments for these same goals are listed in the chart on pages 59 and 60.

Ongoing Assessment Opportunities

Ongoing assessment opportunities are opportunities to observe children during regular interactions, as they work independently and in groups. You can conduct ongoing assessment during teacher-guided instruction, Math Boxes sessions, mathematical mini-interviews, games, Mental Math and Reflexes sessions, strategy sharing, and slate work. The chart below provides a summary of ongoing assessment opportunities in Unit 8, as they relate to specific Unit 8 learning goals.

8a **Beginning Goal** Make change for amounts less than $1. (Lesson 8.5)	Lesson 8.5, p. 637
8b **Beginning/Developing Goal** Identify fractional parts of regions and sets with a focus on unit fractions. (Lessons 8.6–8.9)	Lesson 8.7, p. 646 Lesson 8.8, p. 651
8c **Developing/Secure Goal** Calculate the values of combinations of pennies, nickels, dimes, and quarters. (Lessons 8.1, 8.2, and 8.7)	Lesson 8.1, p. 615 Lesson 8.2, p. 621
8d **Developing/Secure Goal** Solve addition and subtraction number stories. (Lesson 8.4)	Lesson 8.4, p. 633
8e **Developing/Secure Goal** Understand place value for tens and ones. (Lessons 8.1–8.5 and 8.8)	Lesson 8.2, p. 621 Lesson 8.3, p. 626

Product Assessment Opportunities

Math Journals, Math Boxes, activity sheets, masters, Math Logs, and the results of Explorations and Projects all provide product assessment opportunities. On the next page is an example of how you might use a rubric to assess children's ability to find the relationships among pattern blocks.

Lesson 8.9, p. 654

EXPLORATION A **Finding the Relationships Involving Pattern Blocks**

This Exploration activity reviews the material in Lesson 6.7. As children work cooperatively, each child makes his or her own record. You may wish to create your own rubric to evaluate children's work, or use the sample rubric below.

Sample Rubric
Beginning (B) The child has difficulty choosing and arranging pattern blocks on the large shapes and does not understand the relationships between the sizes of the larger and smaller shapes.
Developing (D) The child is able to get started on his or her own but requires assistance to draw the arrangement of pattern blocks on the larger shape. He or she may also require assistance in expressing numerical relationships between the smaller pattern blocks and the larger shape. For example, the child might not understand that if eight small triangles are used to cover the large rhombus, then each triangle is $\frac{1}{8}$ of the rhombus.
Secure (S) The child is able to complete the Exploration successfully by making the drawings and recording the correct numerical relationships among the pattern blocks.

Periodic Assessment Opportunities

Here is a summary of the periodic assessment opportunities that are provided in Unit 8. Refer to Lesson 8.10 for details.

Oral and Slate Assessment

In Lesson 8.10, you will find oral and slate assessment problems on pages 658 and 659.

Written Assessment

In Lesson 8.10, you will find written assessment problems on pages 659 and 660 (*Math Masters,* pages 314 and 315).

See the chart below to find oral, slate, and written assessment problems that address specific learning goals.

8a **Beginning Goal** Make change for amounts less than $1. (Lesson 8.5)	Slate Assessment, Problem 5 Written Assessment, Problem 1
8b **Beginning/Developing Goal** Identify fractional parts of regions and sets with a focus on unit fractions. (Lessons 8.6–8.9)	Slate Assessment, Problem 5 Written Assessment, Problems 9–11
8c **Developing/Secure Goal** Calculate the values of combinations of pennies, nickels, dimes, and quarters. (Lessons 8.1, 8.2, and 8.7)	Oral Assessment, Problem 4 Slate Assessment, Problem 1 Written Assessment, Problems 1 and 2
8d **Developing/Secure Goal** Solve addition and subtraction number stories. (Lesson 8.4)	Slate Assessment, Problem 5 Written Assessment, Problem 12

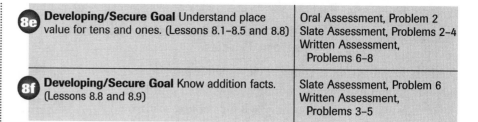

	Developing/Secure Goal Understand place value for tens and ones. (Lessons 8.1–8.5 and 8.8)	Oral Assessment, Problem 2 Slate Assessment, Problems 2–4 Written Assessment, Problems 6–8
8e		
8f	Developing/Secure Goal Know addition facts. (Lessons 8.8 and 8.9)	Slate Assessment, Problem 6 Written Assessment, Problems 3–5

Alternative Assessment

In Lesson 8.10, you will find alternative assessment options on page 660.

✦ **Play** *One-Dollar Exchange*

Circulate and assess children's ability to exchange pennies for dimes and dimes for dollars. Record your observations using either Flip Cards or your Class Checklist.

Watch for the following:

• Are children using the proper symbols to record the amounts?

• Do they use dollars-and-cents notation to write the final amounts?

✦ **Play** *Base-10 Exchange*

To evaluate whether children understand how to use place-value concepts, circulate and examine their drawings to see if children correctly use flats, longs, and cubes to represent the relationships among dollars, dimes, and pennies. Ask them to explain which number each configuration of blocks represents.

✦ **Shop at the Museum Store**

To assess children's progress with making change, ask them to model a shopping trip to a museum store, using the Museum Store Mini-Poster from journal page 189.

Keep questions like the following in mind:

• Were children able to use the proper coins consistently while making change?

• Did children have more difficulty with some coins than with others? Which coins appeared to be the most difficult for children to use correctly?

✦ *Math Journal 2*, p. 189

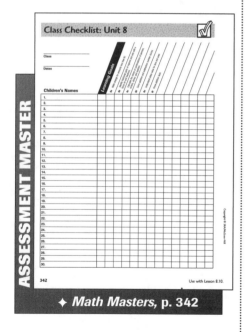

✦ *Math Masters*, p. 342

Unit 9
Assessment Overview

As you near the end of the *First Grade Everyday Mathematics* program, reflect on your success in developing a balanced assessment plan. Think about which assessment strategies worked best and which strategies could be improved. Are there strategies that you did not have time to try this year, but that you would like to try next year? To help you remember them next fall, record your thoughts on the note pages in this book.

Ongoing Assessment Opportunities

Ongoing assessment opportunities are opportunities to observe children during regular interactions, as they work independently and in groups. You can conduct ongoing assessment during teacher-guided instruction, Math Boxes sessions, mathematical mini-interviews, games, Mental Math and Reflexes sessions, strategy sharing, and slate work. The chart below provides a summary of ongoing assessment opportunities in Unit 9, as they relate to specific Unit 9 learning goals.

9a	**Beginning Goal** Solve 2-digit addition and subtraction problems. (Lessons 9.2–9.4)	Lesson 9.2, p. 681
9b	**Beginning Goal** Compare fractions less than 1. (Lesson 9.7)	Lesson 9.7, p. 703
9d	**Beginning/Developing Goal** Identify fractional parts of a region. (Lessons 9.6–9.8)	Lesson 9.8, p. 708
9e	**Developing/Secure Goal** Identify and use patterns on the number grid. (Lessons 9.1–9.4 and 9.7)	Lesson 9.1, p. 677 Lesson 9.2, p. 681

Product Assessment Opportunities

Math Journals, Math Boxes, activity sheets, masters, Math Logs, and the results of Explorations and Projects all provide product assessment opportunities. On the next page is an example of how you might use a rubric to assess children's ability to compare fractions.

Lesson 9.7, p. 705

EXTRA PRACTICE Comparing Fractions

As children work independently on this Extra Practice activity, each child divides hexagons into two, three, and six equal parts and then uses those parts to compare pairs of fractions. As they compare pairs of fractions, children must determine which member of each pair is larger than the other member or whether they are equal. For example, is $\frac{1}{2}$ greater than, less than, or equal to $\frac{2}{3}$? You may wish to create your own rubric to evaluate children's work, or use the sample rubric below.

Sample Rubric
Beginning (B)
The child has difficulty dividing the hexagons into equal parts. He or she can probably divide them into halves but is unable to show thirds or sixths.
Developing (D)
The child is able to divide the hexagons correctly on his or her own but requires assistance using the hexagons to solve problems involving pairs of fractions. For example, the child might be able to visualize that $\frac{1}{6}$ is smaller than $\frac{5}{6}$ but may have difficulty making a comparison between $\frac{1}{3}$ and $\frac{2}{6}$.
Secure (S)
The child is able to complete all drawings successfully and correctly solve the problems with little or no assistance.

Periodic Assessment Opportunities

Here is a summary of the periodic assessment opportunities that are provided in Unit 9. Refer to Lesson 9.9 for details.

Oral and Slate Assessment

In Lesson 9.9, you will find oral and slate assessment problems on pages 712–714.

Written Assessment

In Lesson 9.9, you will find written assessment problems on page 714 (*Math Masters,* pages 316 and 317).

See the chart below and on page 63 to find slate and written assessment problems that address specific learning goals.

9a	**Beginning Goal** Solve 2-digit addition and subtraction problems. (Lessons 9.2–9.4)	Slate Assessment, Problem 5 Written Assessment, Problems 4–7
9b	**Beginning Goal** Compare fractions less than 1. (Lesson 9.7)	Written Assessment, Problems 11–16
9c	**Beginning Goal** Find equivalent fractions for given fractions. (Lesson 9.8)	Slate Assessment, Problem 1 Written Assessment, Problems 11–16

9d **Beginning/Developing Goal** Identify fractional parts of a region. (Lessons 9.6–9.8)	Slate Assessment, Problem 1 Written Assessment, Problems 8–10
9e **Developing/Secure Goal** Identify and use patterns on the number grid. (Lessons 9.1–9.4 and 9.7)	Written Assessment, Problems 1–3

Alternative Assessment

In Lesson 9.9, you will find alternative assessment options on pages 714 and 715.

✦ Complete a Number Grid

Circulate and assess children's ability to complete a number grid. Record your observations using Flip Cards or your Class Checklist.

Watch for the following:

• Are children leaving the 1s digit the same in each column when completing the grid?

• Are children leaving the 10s digit the same in each row (except for the last number) when completing the grid?

✦ Match Fractions

To evaluate whether children are making progress finding equivalent fractions, circulate and look at children's drawings. Record your observations using Flip Cards or your Class Checklist.

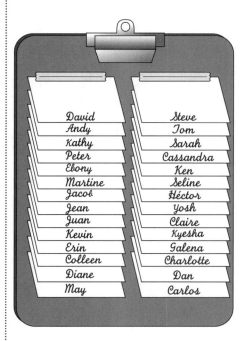

✦ *Math Masters, p. 344*

Assessment Masters

How to Use the Masters

The *Assessment Handbook* contains reduced versions of all of the Assessment Masters found in your *Math Masters* book. You can use these reduced pages to assist you in developing your assessment plan. The following general masters may be adapted in any way to suit your needs; however, the suggestions below may be helpful.

Use the **List of Assessment Sources** to keep track of the sources that you are currently using. As you plan your assessment, aim for the balance of techniques that will meet your children's needs.

On the **Individual Profile of Progress**

- Copy the Learning Goals from the Assessment Lesson at the end of each unit. (See the *Teacher's Lesson Guide.*)
- Make as many copies of the form as you need for each child in your class.
- Keep track of each child's progress on each unit's skills and concepts using this form.
- Check whether each child is Beginning, Developing, or Secure in each of the content areas.
- You may alternatively wish to use the **Class Checklist.**

Make several copies of the **Class Progress Indicator.** Use one page for each mathematical topic being assessed. Fill in the topic you wish to assess under the chart heading and then write each child's name in the appropriate box, indicating whether he or she is Beginning, Developing, or Secure.

The **Parent Reflections** master can be sent to parents prior to parent conferences, so that parents can identify their concerns prior to the meeting.

You can use the **Rubric** master to create your own rubric for a given task, especially for products that will be included in portfolios. Use Beginning, Developing, Secure or your own rubric scheme.

All of the other forms are to be passed out to children. Use the interest inventories to find out how children feel about mathematics. Self-assessment forms should be used as attachments to portfolio items. The remaining forms can provide insight into how comfortable children feel with the math content.

> NOTE: This page provides a brief summary of how the general Assessment Masters may be used. The uses of these masters are described in more detail near the front of this book on pages 5–30.

Unit 2 Checking Progress

Name _____ Date _____

1. What time is it?

_5_ o'clock   _9_ o'clock

2. Draw the hour hand and the minute hand.

4 o'clock   8 o'clock

3. How much money has Dorothy saved? _17_ ¢

Ⓝ Ⓝ Ⓝ Ⓟ Ⓟ

4. How much money has Frank saved? _15_ ¢

Ⓟ Ⓟ Ⓟ Ⓟ Ⓟ Ⓝ

5. How much money has Phyllis saved? _16_ ¢

Ⓟ Ⓝ Ⓟ Ⓟ Ⓝ Ⓟ Ⓟ

Show the same amount with fewer coins.
Draw Ⓟs and Ⓝs on the back of this page.

Use with Lesson 2.14.

304

Unit 1 Checking Progress

Name _____ Date _____

1. Write the number for each set of tally marks.

_8_ = ⵘ ///   _11_ = ⵘ ⵘ /

2. Make tally marks for each number below.

7 = ⵘ //   16 = ⵘ ⵘ ⵘ /

3. Write the number that is 1 more than 15. _16_

4. Circle the number that could be the mystery number in this game of Number-Line Squeeze.

5 6 7 8 9 10 11 12 13 14 15

8 ⑩ 12

5. Circle the winner in this round of *Top-It.*

12   ⑬

6. Write the three numbers from 1 through 6 that you do the best.

_____

Use with Lesson 1.14.

303

Name _____ Date _____

Unit 3 Checking Progress (cont.)

4. Complete the diagrams.

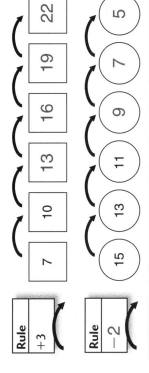

Rule
+3

7 → 10 → 13 → 16 → 19 → 22

Rule
−2

15 → 13 → 11 → 9 → 7 → 5

5. Use your number grid to help you solve these problems.

Start at 25. Count up 3 steps. You end up on __28__ .

$25 + 3 = \underline{28}$

Start at 32. Count back 9 steps. You end up on __23__ .

$32 - 9 = \underline{23}$

$39 + 7 = \underline{46}$

$42 - 5 = \underline{37}$

$45 + 10 = \underline{55}$

$53 - 10 = \underline{43}$

Use with Lesson 3.15.

Name _____ Date _____

Unit 3 Checking Progress

1. Tell the time.

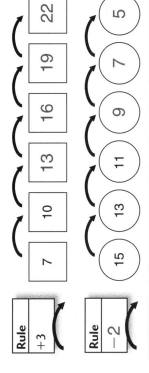

__7__ o'clock   half-past __11__ o'clock

2. Circle the odd numbers.

(5) (7) 12 16 (19) 24 (27) 28 (33)

3. How much money is this?

N N N N N P P P P P __41__ ¢

Show the same amount using fewer coins.
Use P, N, and D.

Fewest coins: D D D D P

How much money is this?

D D N N P P P __38__ ¢

P D P N N P D N N D __53__ ¢

Use with Lesson 3.15.

Name _____ Date _____

Unit 4 Checking Progress

Tell the time.

1.

half-past
__10__ o'clock

2.

quarter-before
__2__ o'clock

Measure to the nearest inch.

3. _____ __2__ inches

4. _____ __3__ inches

5. _____ __5__ inches

6. Draw a line segment that is about 4 inches long.

_____

Use with Lesson 4.13.

307

Name _____ Date _____

Unit 4 Checking Progress (cont.)

7. How much money has Dolores saved?

Ⓓ Ⓓ Ⓝ Ⓝ Ⓝ Ⓟ Ⓟ Ⓟ Ⓟ __45__ ¢

Show the same amount using fewer coins.
Use Ⓟ, Ⓝ, and Ⓓ.
Answers vary.

Write each sum.

8.

$3 + 5 =$ __8__

9.

$4 + 2 =$ __6__

10.

7 __=__ $4 + 3$

11.
$$\begin{array}{r} 5 \\ +6 \\ \hline 11 \end{array}$$

12.
$$\begin{array}{r} 8 \\ +1 \\ \hline 9 \end{array}$$

13.
$$\begin{array}{r} 6 \\ +9 \\ \hline 15 \end{array}$$

Use with Lesson 4.13.

308

Name _____ Date _____

Unit 5 Checking Progress (cont.)

Write <, >, or =.

11. 17 $\le$ 24 **12.** 32 $>$ 23 **13.** 84 $>$ 44 **14.** 51 $<$ 56

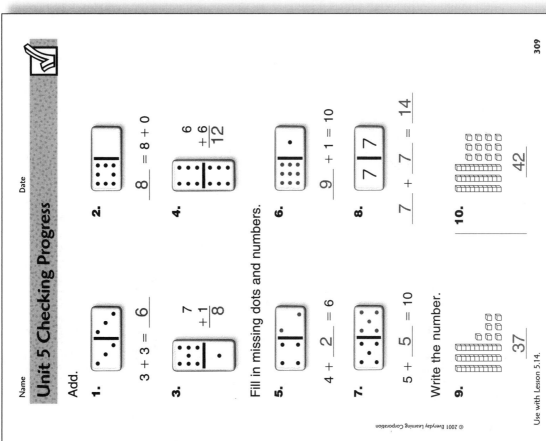

15. Tina (P)(P)(P)(P)(P)(P)(P)(P)

Elise (P)(P)(P)(P)(P)

Who has more? __Tina__

How much more? __3__ ¢

Jerry [26 pennies]

Chris [43 pennies]

Who has more? __Chris__

How much more? __17__ ¢

16. What comes out?

Rule +2

in	out
3	5
12	14
9	11
25	27

17. Find the rule. Fill in the missing numbers.

Rule +10

in	out
4	14
50	60
22	32
55	65
80	90

Use with Lesson 5.14.

310

Name _____ Date _____

Unit 5 Checking Progress

Add.

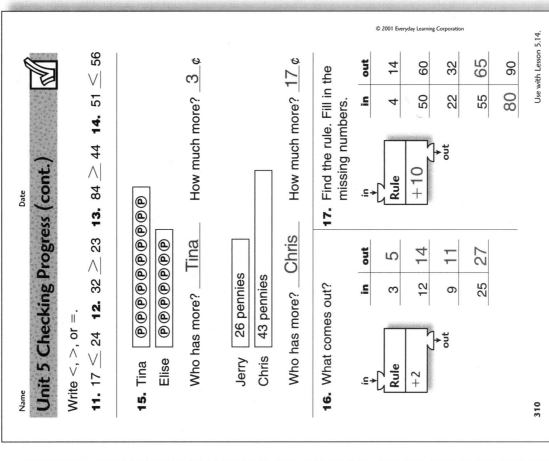

1. 3 + 3 = __6__

2. __8__ = 8 + 0

3. 7 + 1 = __8__

4. 6 + 6 = __12__

Fill in missing dots and numbers.

5. 4 + __2__ = 6

6. 9 + 1 = 10

7. 5 + __5__ = 10

8. 7 | 7   7 + 7 = __14__

Write the number.

9. __37__

10. __42__

Use with Lesson 5.14.

309

Name _____ Date _____

Unit 7 Checking Progress

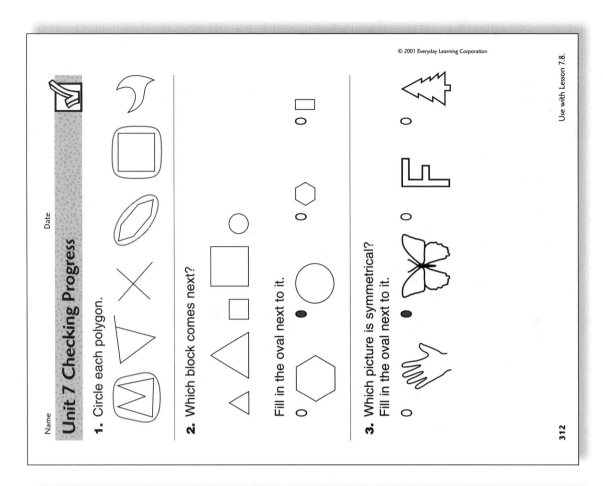

1. Circle each polygon.

2. Which block comes next?

Fill in the oval next to it.

3. Which picture is symmetrical?
Fill in the oval next to it.

Use with Lesson 7.8.

312

Name _____ Date _____

Unit 6 Checking Progress

Tell the time.

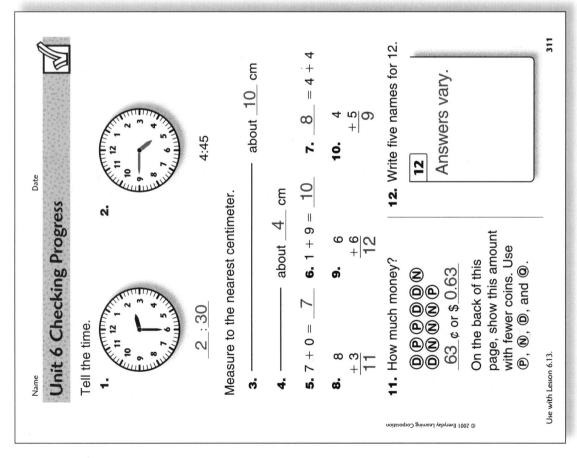

1.

2.

2 : 30   4:45

Measure to the nearest centimeter.

3. _____ about __10__ cm

4. _____ about __4__ cm

5. $7 + 0 =$ __7__   **6.** $1 + 9 =$ __10__   **7.** __8__ $= 4 + 4$

8. 8
  + 3
  ‾‾‾
  11

9. 6
  + 6
  ‾‾‾
  12

10. 4
  + 5
  ‾‾‾
  9

11. How much money?

Ⓓ Ⓟ Ⓟ Ⓓ Ⓓ Ⓝ
Ⓓ Ⓝ Ⓝ Ⓟ

__63__ ¢ or $ __0.63__

On the back of this
page, show this amount
with fewer coins. Use
Ⓟ, Ⓝ, Ⓓ, and Ⓠ.

12. Write five names for 12.

12

Answers vary.

311

Use with Lesson 6.13.

Name _____ Date _____

Unit 7 Checking Progress (cont.)

4. Circle the cylinder.
Put an X through the pyramid.

5. Complete the Fact Triangle.
Then write the fact family. Order may vary.

$2 + 7 = 9$

$7 + 2 = 9$

$9 - 2 = 7$

$9 - 7 = 2$

Use with Lesson 7.8.

Name _____ Date _____

Unit 8 Checking Progress

1. Mark the coins you need to buy a toy dinosaur.
Answers vary.

74¢

If you pay for the dinosaur with 8 dimes,
how much change would you get back? __6¢__

2. Draw bills and coins to show the amount you need
to buy the book.

MYSTERY

$1.85

Answers vary.

Fill in the missing numbers.

3. $3 + \underline{7} = 10$ **4.** $14 = 7 + \underline{7}$ **5.** $1 + \underline{8} = 9$

Use with Lesson 8.10.

Name _____ Date _____

Unit 9 Checking Progress

Complete the number-grid puzzles below.

1.

18
28
38
48
58
68

2.

34	
44	45
	55
	65
74	

3.

60	
	71	62
	81	
	91	
		102

4. 35 + 10 = __45__   **5.** 27 − 20 = __7__

6. How much do the raccoon and the koala weigh together?

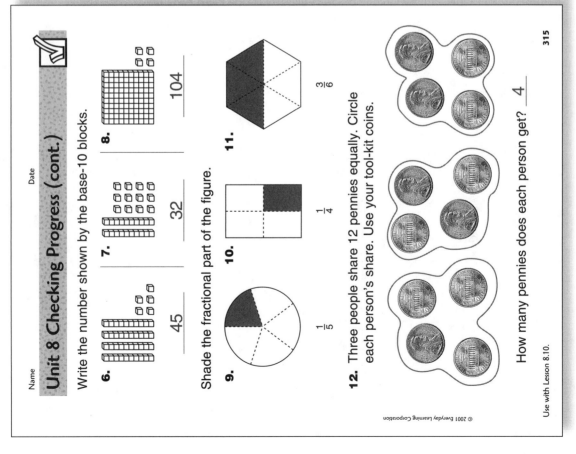

23 lb   19 lb

__42__ pounds

7. How much longer is the cheetah than the rabbit?

57 in.   11 in.

__46__ inches

316

© 2001 Everyday Learning Corporation

Use with Lesson 9.9.

Name _____ Date _____

Unit 8 Checking Progress (cont.)

Write the number shown by the base-10 blocks.

6.

__45__

7.

__32__

8.

__104__

Shade the fractional part of the figure.

9.

$\frac{1}{5}$

10.

$\frac{1}{4}$

11.

$\frac{3}{6}$

12. Three people share 12 pennies equally. Circle each person's share. Use your tool-kit coins.

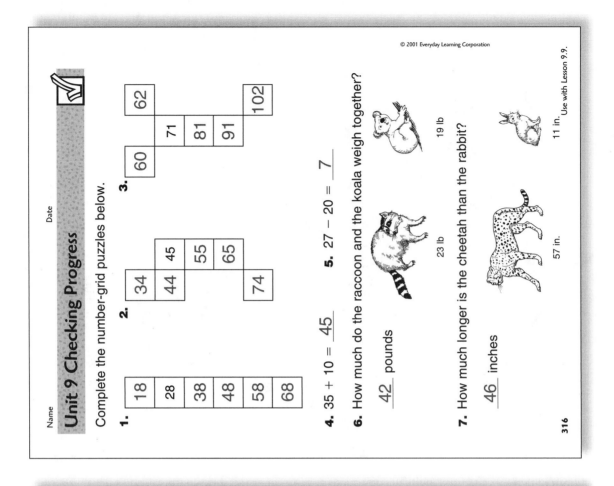

How many pennies does each person get? __4__

Use with Lesson 8.10.

315

© 2001 Everyday Learning Corporation

---

72   Assessment Handbook

Name _____ Date _____

Midyear Assessment

1. Make a tally for each number below.

28 //// //// //// //// //// ///

36 //// //// //// //// //// //// //// /

2. Complete the table.

Before	Number	After
14	15	16
19	20	21
40	41	42
78	79	80
100	101	102

3. Fill in the frames.

Rule
+2

10 → 12 → 14 → 16 → 18 → 20

Use with Lesson 5.14.

318

Name _____ Date _____

Unit 9 Checking Progress (cont.)

Use your template to divide the hexagons.

8. Halves — Shade $\frac{1}{2}$ of the hexagon.

9. Thirds — Shade $\frac{2}{3}$ of the hexagon.

10. Sixths — Shade $\frac{5}{6}$ of the hexagon.

Write >, <, or =.

Hint: Use Problems 8–10 to help you.

< is less than
> is greater than
= is equal to

11. $\frac{1}{2}$ < $\frac{2}{3}$

12. $\frac{1}{2}$ > $\frac{1}{3}$

13. $\frac{1}{3}$ < $\frac{5}{6}$

14. $\frac{2}{3}$ = $\frac{4}{6}$

15. $\frac{3}{6}$ = $\frac{1}{2}$

16. $\frac{5}{6}$ > $\frac{2}{3}$

Use with Lesson 9.9.

317

Name _____ Date _____

Midyear Assessment (cont.)

4. Fill in the frames.

Rule	
+5	

25 → 30 → 35 → 40 → 45 → 50

5. Find the rule. Fill in the frames.

Rule	
+2	

43 → 45 → 47 → 49 → 51 → 53

6. Draw the hands.

5 o'clock

half-past
3 o'clock

half-past
11 o'clock

Use with Lesson 5.14.

319

Name _____ Date _____

Midyear Assessment (cont.)

7. Write the missing numbers.

$$\begin{array}{r} 4 \\ +2 \\ \hline 6 \end{array} \qquad \begin{array}{r} 2 \\ +2 \\ \hline 4 \end{array} \qquad \begin{array}{r} 5 \\ +1 \\ \hline 6 \end{array}$$

$3 + 3 = \underline{6}$ $\qquad$ $\underline{7} = 1 + 6$ $\qquad$ $\underline{10} = 2 + 8$

8.  D D N N N N P P P

How much money is this? $\underline{48}$ ¢

Show the same amount using fewer coins.

Sample answer: D D D D N P P P

9. P D N N P P P D P N

How much money is this? $\underline{40}$ ¢, or $ $\underline{0.40}$

Show the same amount using fewer coins.

Sample answer: D D D D

320

Use with Lesson 5.14.

Name _____ Date _____

End-of-Year Assessment (cont.)

4. Use Ⓟ, Ⓝ, Ⓓ, and Ⓠ to show the coins you need to buy the crayons.

78¢

Sample answer: Ⓠ Ⓠ Ⓟ Ⓟ Ⓟ

Show this amount another way.

Sample answer: Ⓠ Ⓠ Ⓓ Ⓓ Ⓝ Ⓟ Ⓟ

5. Fill in the circle next to the name of each shape.

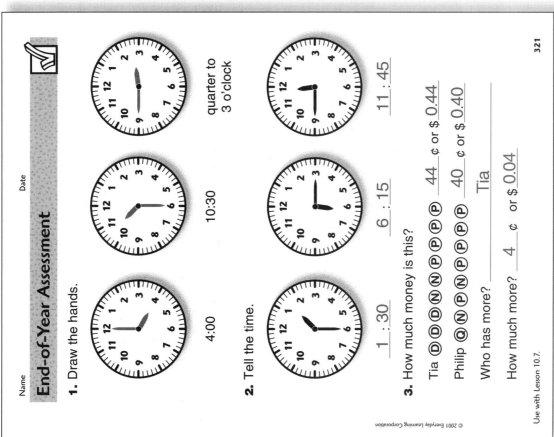

○ circle
○ square
○ triangle
● rectangle

○ circle
● triangle
○ hexagon
○ square

● circle
○ rectangle
○ square
○ triangle

○ circle
○ sphere
● cone
○ triangle

322   Use with Lesson 10.7.

Name _____ Date _____

End-of-Year Assessment

1. Draw the hands.

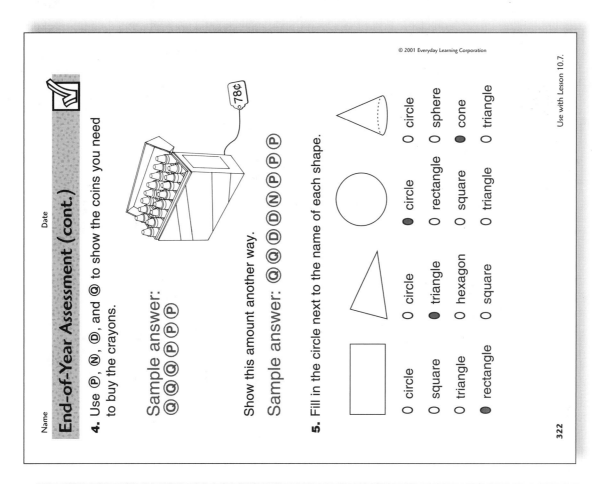

4:00   10:30   quarter to 3 o'clock

2. Tell the time.

1 : 30   6 : 15   11 : 45

3. How much money is this?

Tia   Ⓓ Ⓓ Ⓝ Ⓝ Ⓟ Ⓟ Ⓟ Ⓟ   __44__ ¢ or $ 0.44

Philip   Ⓠ Ⓝ Ⓟ Ⓝ Ⓟ Ⓟ Ⓟ Ⓟ   __40__ ¢ or $ 0.40

Who has more?   __Tia__

How much more?   __4__ ¢ or $ 0.04

Name _____ Date _____

End-of-Year Assessment (cont.)

6. Fill in the missing numbers.

6 + __2__ = 8   10 = 5 + __5__

+ 6
―――
12 → **6**

+ 0
―――
4 → **4**

7. Complete the fact triangle and write the fact family.

10
7   3
+, −

3 + __7__ = __10__

7 + __3__ = __10__

10 − __3__ = __7__

10 − __7__ = __3__

8. Fill in the missing numbers.

Rule: +10

⬡ 70 → ⬡ 80 → ⬡ 90 → ⬡ 100 → ⬡ 110 → ⬡ 120

9. Find the rule. Fill in the missing numbers.

Rule: −2

☐ 34 → ☐ 32 → ☐ 30 → ☐ 28 → ☐ 26 → ☐ 24

Name _____ Date _____

End-of-Year Assessment (cont.)

10. Find the rule and complete the table.

in → Rule: −3 → out

in	out
8	5
23	20
30	27
55	52

Answers vary.

11. Write 6 names for 30.

30

Sample answers:

10 + 20

29 + 1

10 + 10 + 10

40 − 10

15 + 15

treinta

12. Measure the line segment to the nearest inch.

_____ about __2__ inches

Draw a line segment that is about 2 inches longer.

_____

How long is this line segment? about __4__ inches

13. Measure each line segment to the nearest half-inch.

_____ about __1½__ inches

_____ about __3__ inches

Name _____ Date _____

End-of-Year Assessment (cont.)

14. Measure each line segment to the nearest centimeter.

_____ about __6__ cm

_____ about __3__ cm

15. Solve the following problems. You may use your number grid.

$18 + 5 = $ __23__ $31 = 24 + 7$ $28 = 31 - 3$

$\begin{array}{r} 38 \\ -2 \\ \hline 36 \end{array}$ $\begin{array}{r} 67 \\ +20 \\ \hline 87 \end{array}$ $\begin{array}{r} 26 \\ -15 \\ \hline 11 \end{array}$

16. Use $>$, $<$, or $=$.

$42 \; > \; 24$

$23 \; > \; 10 + 10$

$81 \; > \; 29$

$4 + 6 \; = \; 7 + 3$

$57 \; < \; 107$

$\$0.32 \; < \; $ ⓓ ⓓ ⓝ ⓓ

17. Complete the number grid puzzle.

58
68
78
88
98
108

Use with Lesson 10.7.

325

Name _____ Date _____

End-of-Year Assessment (cont.)

18. How much more does the raccoon weigh than the rabbit?

raccoon
23 lb

rabbit
6 lb

about __17__ pounds

19. Write the numbers shown by base-10 blocks. Circle the right word to tell if the number is odd or even.

__32__
odd or (even)

__38__
odd or (even)

__103__
(odd) or even

20. Write these numbers.

3 tens 5 ones   17 ones 8 tens   4 hundreds 2 tens

__35__   __97__   __420__

Use with Lesson 10.7.

326

Class Checklist: Unit 1

Class _____

Dates _____

Learning Goals

1a	Count by 5s to 40.
1b	Count by 2s to 40.
1c	Write numbers from 1 to 20.
1d	Compare pairs of numbers less than 16.
1e	Write and count tallies.
1f	Count up and back by 1s, starting with any number up to and including 20.
1g	Count 20 or more objects.

Children's Names

1.
2.
3.
4.
5.
6.
7.
8.
9.
10.
11.
12.
13.
14.
15.
16.
17.
18.
19.
20.
21.
22.
23.
24.
25.
26.
27.
28.
29.
30.

Use with Lesson 1.14.

328

Name _____ Date _____

End-of-Year Assessment (cont.)

21. Shade the fraction for each shape.

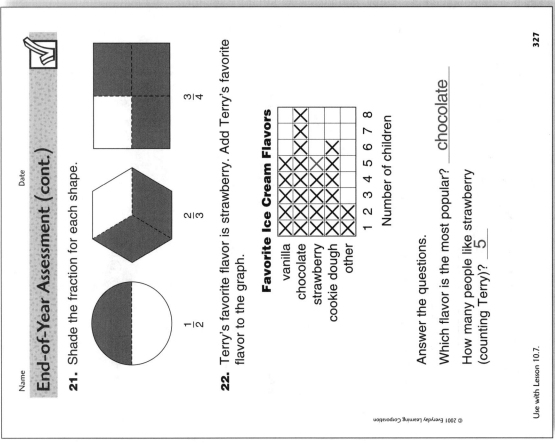

$\frac{1}{2}$ $\frac{2}{3}$ $\frac{3}{4}$

22. Terry's favorite flavor is strawberry. Add Terry's favorite flavor to the graph.

Favorite Ice Cream Flavors

vanilla
chocolate
strawberry
cookie dough
other

1 2 3 4 5 6 7 8
Number of children

Answer the questions.

Which flavor is the most popular? __chocolate__

How many people like strawberry (counting Terry)? __5__

Use with Lesson 10.7.

327

Class Checklist: Unit 2

Class _____

Dates _____

Learning Goals

2a Calculate the values of combinations of pennies and nickels.

2b Find complements of 10.

2c Solve addition and subtraction number stories.

2d Count up and back by 1s on the number grid.

2e Tell time to the nearest hour.

2f Exchange pennies for nickels.

2g Count by 2s to 40. Count by 5s to 50.

Children's Names

1.
2.
3.
4.
5.
6.
7.
8.
9.
10.
11.
12.
13.
14.
15.
16.
17.
18.
19.
20.
21.
22.
23.
24.
25.
26.
27.
28.
29.
30.

Use with Lesson 2.14.

330

Child's Name _____   Date _____

Individual Profile of Progress: Unit 1

Check ✔			Learning Goals	Comments
B	D	S		
			1a Count by 5s to 40.	
			1b Count by 2s to 40.	
			1c Write numbers from 1 to 20.	
			1d Compare pairs of numbers less than 16.	
			1e Write and count tallies.	
			1f Count up and back by 1s, starting with any number up to and including 20.	
			1g Count 20 or more objects.	

Notes to Parents

_____

_____

_____

B = Beginning; **D** = Developing; **S** = Secure

Use with Lesson 1.14.

329

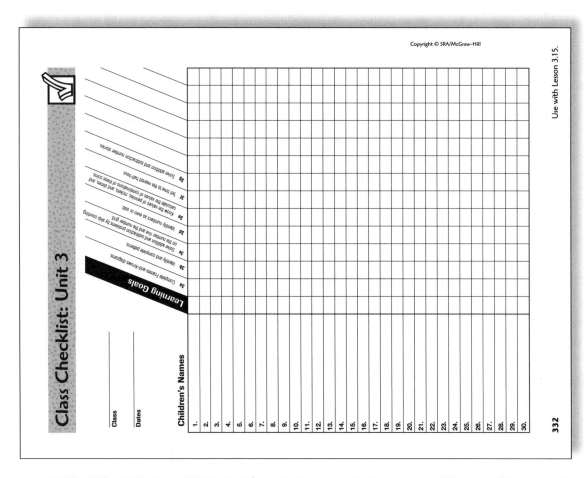

Class Checklist: Unit 3

Copyright © SRA/McGraw–Hill

Class _____

Dates _____

Learning Goals

- **3a** Complete Frames-and-Arrows diagrams.
- **3b** Identify and complete patterns.
- **3c** Solve addition and subtraction problems by skip counting on the number line and the number grid.
- **3d** Identify numbers as even or odd.
- **3e** Know the values of pennies, nickels, and dimes, and calculate the values of combinations of these coins.
- **3f** Tell time to the nearest half-hour.
- **3g** Solve addition and subtraction number stories.

Children's Names

1. 2. 3. 4. 5. 6. 7. 8. 9. 10. 11. 12. 13. 14. 15. 16. 17. 18. 19. 20. 21. 22. 23. 24. 25. 26. 27. 28. 29. 30.

Use with Lesson 3.15.

332

Child's Name _____ Date _____

Individual Profile of Progress: Unit 2

Check ✔			Learning Goals	Comments
B	**D**	**S**		
			2a Calculate the values of combinations of pennies and nickels.	
			2b Find complements of 10.	
			2c Solve addition and subtraction number stories.	
			2d Count up and back by 1s on the number grid.	
			2e Tell time to the nearest hour.	
			2f Exchange pennies for nickels.	
			2g Count by 2s to 40. Count by 5s to 50.	

Notes to Parents

B = Beginning; **D** = Developing; **S** = Secure

Use with Lesson 2.14.

331

Class Checklist: Unit 4

Class _____

Dates _____

Learning Goals

4a Use standard units for measuring length.
4b Find sums and missing addends.
4c Calculate the values of combinations of pennies, nickels, and dimes.
4d Solve addition and subtraction number stories.
4e Order and compare numbers to 22.
4f Tell time to the nearest half-hour.

Children's Names

1.
2.
3.
4.
5.
6.
7.
8.
9.
10.
11.
12.
13.
14.
15.
16.
17.
18.
19.
20.
21.
22.
23.
24.
25.
26.
27.
28.
29.
30.

Use with Lesson 4.13.

334

Child's Name _____   Date _____

Individual Profile of Progress: Unit 3

Check ✔			Learning Goals	Comments
B	D	S		
			3a Complete Frames-and-Arrows diagrams.	
			3b Identify and complete patterns.	
			3c Solve addition and subtraction problems by skip counting on the number line and the number grid.	
			3d Identify numbers as even or odd.	
			3e Know the values of pennies, nickels, and dimes, and calculate the values of combinations of these coins.	
			3f Tell time to the nearest half-hour.	
			3g Solve addition and subtraction number stories.	

Notes to Parents

_____

_____

_____

B = Beginning; D = Developing; S = Secure

Use with Lesson 3.15.

333

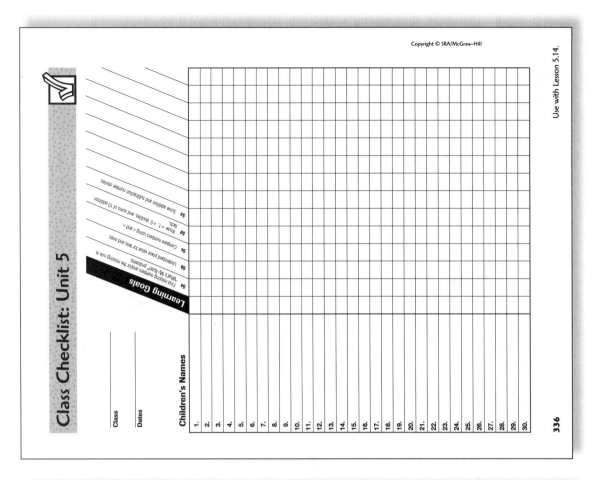

Class Checklist: Unit 5

Class _____

Dates _____ _____

Learning Goals

- 5a Find missing numbers and/or the missing rule in "What's My Rule?" problems.
- 5b Understand place value for tens and ones.
- 5c Compare numbers using < and >.
- 5d Know +1, +0, doubles, and sums of 10 addition facts.
- 5e Solve addition and subtraction number stories.

Children's Names

1.
2.
3.
4.
5.
6.
7.
8.
9.
10.
11.
12.
13.
14.
15.
16.
17.
18.
19.
20.
21.
22.
23.
24.
25.
26.
27.
28.
29.
30.

336   Use with Lesson 5.14.

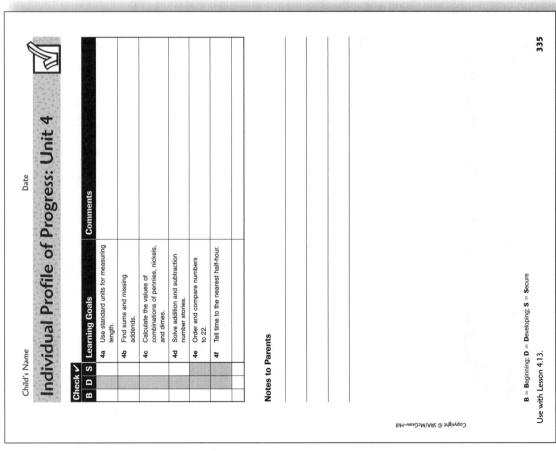

Child's Name _____   Date _____

Individual Profile of Progress: Unit 4

Check ✔			Learning Goals	Comments
B	D	S		
			4a Use standard units for measuring length.	
			4b Find sums and missing addends.	
			4c Calculate the values of combinations of pennies, nickels, and dimes.	
			4d Solve addition and subtraction number stories.	
			4e Order and compare numbers to 22.	
			4f Tell time to the nearest half-hour.	

Notes to Parents

B = Beginning; D = Developing; S = Secure

Use with Lesson 4.13.

335

Class Checklist: Unit 6

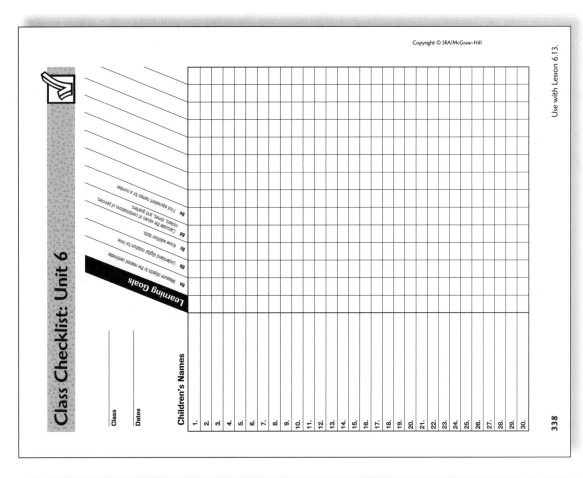

Class _____

Dates _____

Learning Goals

- **6a** Measure objects to the nearest centimeter.
- **6b** Understand digital notation for time.
- **6c** Know addition facts.
- **6d** Calculate the values of combinations of pennies, nickels, dimes, and quarters.
- **6e** Find equivalent names for a number.

Children's Names

1.
2.
3.
4.
5.
6.
7.
8.
9.
10.
11.
12.
13.
14.
15.
16.
17.
18.
19.
20.
21.
22.
23.
24.
25.
26.
27.
28.
29.
30.

Use with Lesson 6.13.

338

Child's Name _____   Date _____

Individual Profile of Progress: Unit 5

Check ✔			Learning Goals	Comments
B	D	S		
			5a Find missing numbers and/or the missing rule in "What's My Rule?" problems.	
			5b Understand place value for tens and ones.	
			5c Compare numbers using < and >.	
			5d Know +1, +0, doubles, and sums of 10 addition facts.	
			5e Solve addition and subtraction number stories.	

Notes to Parents

_____

_____

_____

_____

B = Beginning; D = Developing; S = Secure

Use with Lesson 5.14.

337

Class Checklist: Unit 7

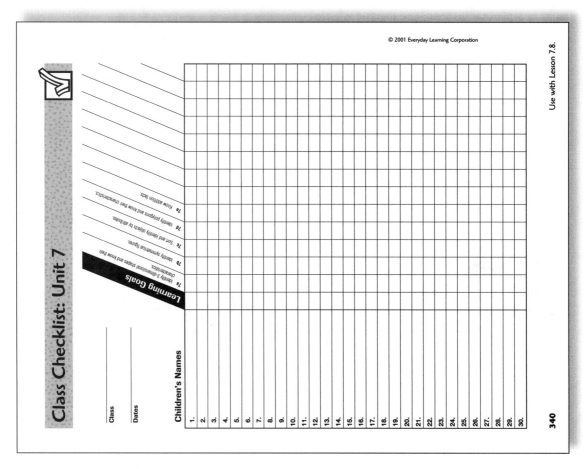

© 2001 Everyday Learning Corporation

Class

Dates

Learning Goals

- 7a Identify 3-dimensional shapes and know their characteristics.
- 7b Identify symmetrical figures.
- 7c Sort and identify objects by attributes.
- 7d Identify polygons and know their characteristics.
- 7e Know addition facts.

Children's Names

1.
2.
3.
4.
5.
6.
7.
8.
9.
10.
11.
12.
13.
14.
15.
16.
17.
18.
19.
20.
21.
22.
23.
24.
25.
26.
27.
28.
29.
30.

340

Use with Lesson 7.8.

Child's Name _____ Date _____

Individual Profile of Progress: Unit 6

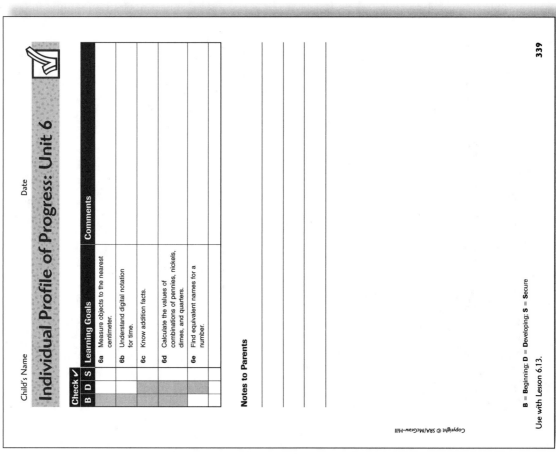

Check ✔			Learning Goals	Comments
B	D	S		
			6a Measure objects to the nearest centimeter.	
			6b Understand digital notation for time.	
			6c Know addition facts.	
			6d Calculate the values of combinations of pennies, nickels, dimes, and quarters.	
			6e Find equivalent names for a number.	

Notes to Parents

B = Beginning; D = Developing; S = Secure

Use with Lesson 6.13.

339

Class Checklist: Unit 8

Class

Dates

Learning Goals

8a Make change for amounts less than $1.

8b Identify fractional parts of regions and sets with a focus on unit fractions.

8c Calculate the values of combinations of pennies, nickels, dimes, and quarters.

8d Solve addition and subtraction number stories.

8e Understand place value for tens and ones.

8f Know addition facts.

Children's Names

1.
2.
3.
4.
5.
6.
7.
8.
9.
10.
11.
12.
13.
14.
15.
16.
17.
18.
19.
20.
21.
22.
23.
24.
25.
26.
27.
28.
29.
30.

Use with Lesson 8.10.

342

Child's Name

Date

Individual Profile of Progress: Unit 7

Check ✔			Learning Goals	Comments
B	D	S		
			7a Identify 3-dimensional shapes and know their characteristics.	
			7b Identify symmetrical figures.	
			7c Sort and identify objects by attributes.	
			7d Identify polygons and know their characteristics.	
			7e Know addition facts.	

Notes to Parents

B = Beginning; **D** = Developing; **S** = Secure

Use with Lesson 7.8.

341

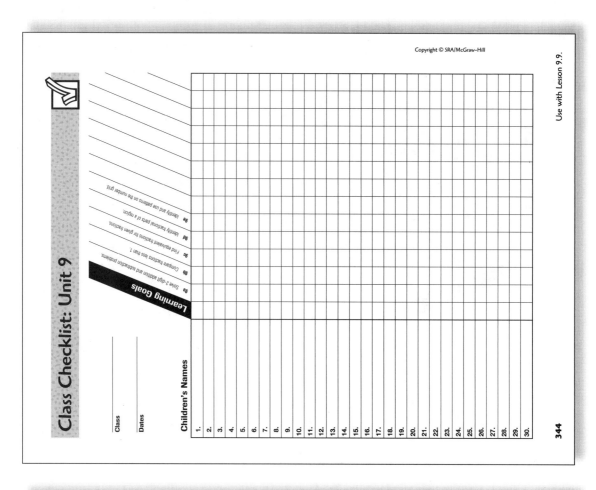

Class Checklist: Unit 9

Class _____

Dates _____

Learning Goals

9a Solve 2-digit addition and subtraction problems.
9b Compare fractions less than 1.
9c Find equivalent fractions for given fractions.
9d Identify fractional parts of a region.
9e Identify and use patterns on the number grid.

Children's Names

1.
2.
3.
4.
5.
6.
7.
8.
9.
10.
11.
12.
13.
14.
15.
16.
17.
18.
19.
20.
21.
22.
23.
24.
25.
26.
27.
28.
29.
30.

Use with Lesson 9.9.

344

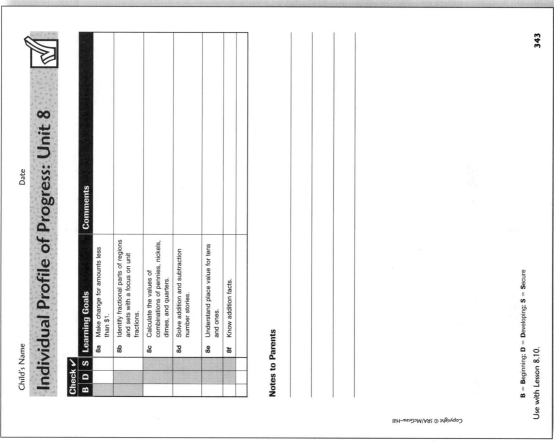

Child's Name _____ Date _____

Individual Profile of Progress: Unit 8

Check ✓
B	D	S		Learning Goals	Comments
			8a	Make change for amounts less than $1.	
			8b	Identify fractional parts of regions and sets with a focus on unit fractions.	
			8c	Calculate the values of combinations of pennies, nickels, dimes, and quarters.	
			8d	Solve addition and subtraction number stories.	
			8e	Understand place value for tens and ones.	
			8f	Know addition facts.	

Notes to Parents

_____

_____

_____

_____

B = Beginning; **D** = Developing; **S** = Secure

Use with Lesson 8.10.

343

Class Checklist: 1st Quarter

Class _____

Dates _____

Learning Goals

1. Count by 5s to 40. (1a)
2. Count by 2s to 40. (1b)
3. Count by 5s to 40. Count by 5s to 50. (2a)
4. Count up and back by 1s, starting with any number up to and including 20. (1f)
5. Count up and back by 1s on the number grid. (2d)
6. Count 20 or more objects. (1g)
7. Write numbers from 1 to 20. (1c)
8. Write and count tallies. (1e)
9. Compare pairs of numbers less than 16. (1d)
10. Find complements of 10. (2b)
11. Solve addition and subtraction number stories. (2c)
12. Calculate the values of combinations of pennies and nickels. (2a)
13. Exchange pennies for nickels. (2c)
14. Tell time to the nearest hour. (2e)

Children's Names

1.
2.
3.
4.
5.
6.
7.
8.
9.
10.
11.
12.
13.
14.
15.
16.
17.
18.
19.
20.
21.
22.
23.
24.
25.
26.
27.
28.
29.
30.

346

Use with Lesson 2.14.

Child's Name _____ Date _____

Individual Profile of Progress: Unit 9

Check ✔			Learning Goals	Comments
B	D	S		
			9a Solve 2-digit addition and subtraction problems.	
			9b Compare fractions less than 1.	
			9c Find equivalent fractions for given fractions.	
			9d Identify fractional parts of a region.	
			9e Identify and use patterns on the number grid.	

Notes to Parents

B = Beginning; D = Developing; S = Secure

Use with Lesson 9.9.

345

Class Checklist: 2nd Quarter

Class _____

Dates _____

Learning Goals

1. Complete Frames-and-Arrows diagrams. **(3a)**
2. Identify and complete patterns. **(3b)**
3. Solve addition and subtraction problems by skip counting on the number line and the number grid. **(3c)**
4. Find sums and missing addends. **(1b)**
5. Know +1, +0 doubles, and sums of 10 addition facts. **(5d)**
6. Find missing numbers and/or the missing rule in "What's My Rule?" problems. **(5a)**
7. Identify numbers as even or odd. **(2d)**
8. Order and compare numbers to 22. **(4e)**
9. Compare numbers using > and <. **(2g)**
10. Understand place value for tens and ones. **(5b)**
11. Solve addition and subtraction number stories. **(3a, 4d, 5a)**
12. Know the values of pennies, nickels, and dimes, and calculate the values of combinations of these coins. **(2c, 4c)**
13. Use standard units for measuring length. **(3e, 4b)**
14. Tell time to the nearest half-hour. **(3f, 4f)**

Children's Names

1.
2.
3.
4.
5.
6.
7.
8.
9.
10.
11.
12.
13.
14.
15.
16.
17.
18.
19.
20.
21.
22.
23.
24.
25.
26.
27.
28.
29.
30.

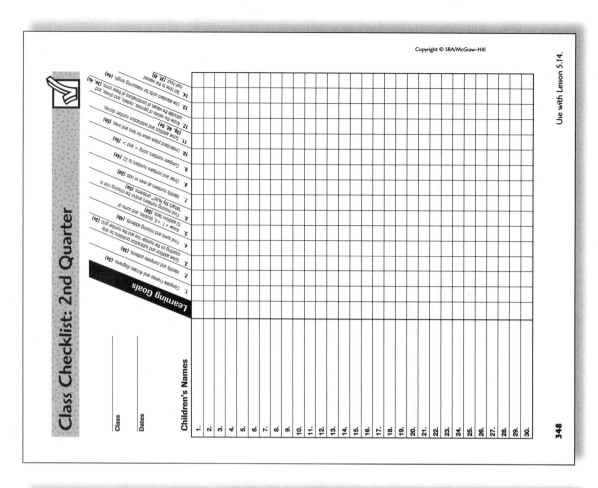

Use with Lesson 5.14.

348

Child's Name _____   Date _____

Individual Profile of Progress: 1st Quarter

Check ✓			Learning Goals	Comments
B	**D**	**S**		
			1. Count by 5s to 40. **(1a)**	
			2. Count by 2s to 40. **(1b)**	
			3. Count by 2s to 40. Count by 5s to 50. **(2g)**	
			4. Count up and back by 1s, starting with any number up to and including 20. **(1f)**	
			5. Count up and back by 1s on the number grid. **(2d)**	
			6. Count 20 or more objects. **(1g)**	
			7. Write numbers from 1 to 20. **(1c)**	
			8. Write and count tallies. **(1e)**	
			9. Compare pairs of numbers less than 16. **(1d)**	
			10. Find complements of 10. **(2b)**	
			11. Solve addition and subtraction number stories. **(2c)**	
			12. Calculate the values of combinations of pennies and nickels. **(2a)**	
			13. Exchange pennies for nickels. **(2f)**	
			14. Tell time to the nearest hour. **(2e)**	

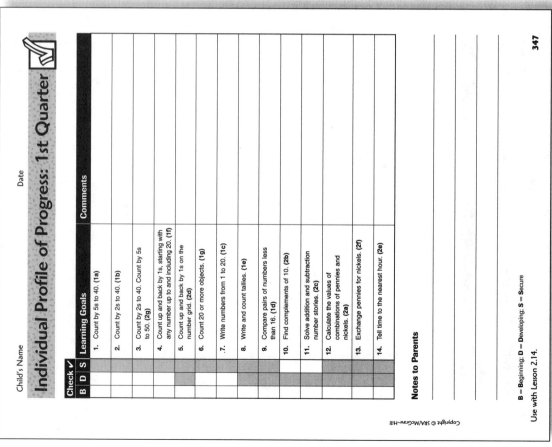

Notes to Parents

B = Beginning; **D** = Developing; **S** = Secure

Use with Lesson 2.14.

347

Class Checklist: 3rd Quarter

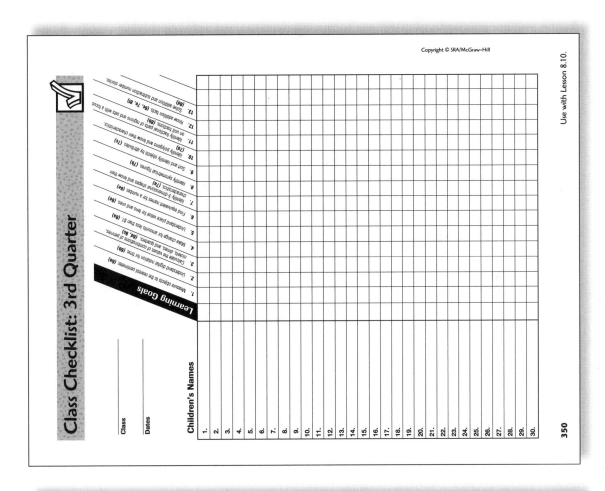

Class _____

Dates _____

Learning Goals

1. Measure objects to the nearest centimeter. (8g)
2. Understand digital notation for time. (6a)
3. Calculate the values of combinations of pennies, nickels, dimes, and quarters. (8d, 8c)
4. Make change for amounts less than $1. (8b)
5. Understand place value for tens and ones. (9a)
6. Find equivalent names for a number. (6c)
7. Identify 3-dimensional shapes and know their characteristics. (7a)
8. Identify symmetrical figures. (7b)
9. Sort and identify objects by attributes. (7c)
10. Identify polygons and know their characteristics. (7d)
11. Identify fractional parts of regions and sets with a focus on unit fractions. (6b)
12. Know addition facts. (6a, 7e, 8i)
13. Solve addition and subtraction number stories. (8d)

Children's Names

1.
2.
3.
4.
5.
6.
7.
8.
9.
10.
11.
12.
13.
14.
15.
16.
17.
18.
19.
20.
21.
22.
23.
24.
25.
26.
27.
28.
29.
30.

Use with Lesson 8.10.

350

Child's Name _____ Date _____

Individual Profile of Progress: 2nd Quarter

Check ✔			Learning Goals	Comments
B	**D**	**S**		
			1. Complete Frames-and-Arrows diagrams. (3a)	
			2. Identify and complete patterns. (3b)	
			3. Solve addition and subtraction problems by skip counting on the number line and the number grid. (3c)	
			4. Find sums and missing addends. (4b)	
			5. Know +1, +0, doubles, and sums of 10 addition facts. (5d)	
			6. Find missing numbers and/or the missing rule in "What's My Rule?" problems. (5a)	
			7. Identify numbers as even or odd. (3d)	
			8. Order and compare numbers to 22. (4e)	
			9. Compare numbers using < and >. (5c)	
			10. Understand place value for tens and ones. (5b)	
			11. Solve addition and subtraction number stories. (3g, 4d, 5e)	
			12. Know the values of pennies, nickels, and dimes, and calculate the values of combinations of these coins. (3e, 4c)	
			13. Use standard units for measuring length. (4a)	
			14. Tell time to the nearest half-hour. (3f, 4f)	

Notes to Parents

_____

_____

_____

B = Beginning; D = Developing; S = Secure

Use with Lesson 5.14.

349

Class Checklist: 4th Quarter

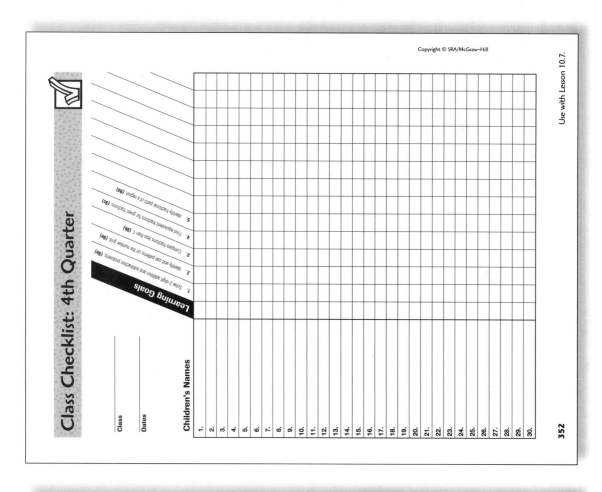

Class _____

Dates _____

Learning Goals

1. Solve 2-digit addition and subtraction problems. (9a)
2. Identify and use patterns on the number grid. (9b)
3. Compare fractions less than 1. (9f)
4. Find equivalent fractions for given fractions. (9e)
5. Identify fractional parts of a region. (9d)

Children's Names

1.
2.
3.
4.
5.
6.
7.
8.
9.
10.
11.
12.
13.
14.
15.
16.
17.
18.
19.
20.
21.
22.
23.
24.
25.
26.
27.
28.
29.
30.

Use with Lesson 10.7.

352

Child's Name _____   Date _____

Individual Profile of Progress: 3rd Quarter

Check ✓			Learning Goals	Comments
B	D	S		
			1. Measure objects to the nearest centimeter. (6a)	
			2. Understand digital notation for time. (6b)	
			3. Calculate the values of combinations of pennies, nickels, dimes, and quarters. (6d, 8c)	
			4. Make change for amounts less than $1. (8a)	
			5. Understand place value for tens and ones. (8e)	
			6. Find equivalent names for a number. (6e)	
			7. Identify 3-dimensional shapes and know their characteristics. (7a)	
			8. Identify symmetrical figures. (7b)	
			9. Sort and identify objects by attributes. (7c)	
			10. Identify polygons and know their characteristics. (7d)	
			11. Identify fractional parts of regions and sets with a focus on unit fractions. (8b)	
			12. Know addition facts. (6c, 7e, 8f)	
			13. Solve addition and subtraction number stories. (8d)	

Notes to Parents

B = **B**eginning; D = **D**eveloping; S = **S**ecure

Use with Lesson 8.10.

351

List of Assessment Sources

Ongoing Assessment

Product Assessment

Periodic Assessment

Outside Tests

Other

Use as needed.

354

Child's Name

Date

Individual Profile of Progress: 4th Quarter

Check ✔			Learning Goals	Comments
B	D	S		
			1. Solve 2-digit addition and subtraction problems. **(9a)**	
			2. Identify and use patterns on the number grid. **(9e)**	
			3. Compare fractions less than 1. **(9b)**	
			4. Find equivalent fractions for given fractions. **(9c)**	
			5. Identify fractional parts of a region. **(9d)**	

Notes to Parents

B = Beginning; **D** = Developing; **S** = Secure

Use with Lesson 10.7.

353

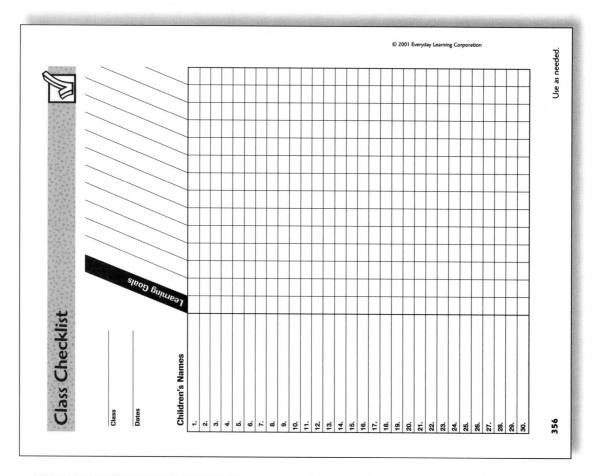

Class Checklist

Class _____

Dates _____

Learning Goals

Children's Names

1.
2.
3.
4.
5.
6.
7.
8.
9.
10.
11.
12.
13.
14.
15.
16.
17.
18.
19.
20.
21.
22.
23.
24.
25.
26.
27.
28.
29.
30.

Use as needed.

356

Child's Name _____   Date _____

Individual Profile of Progress

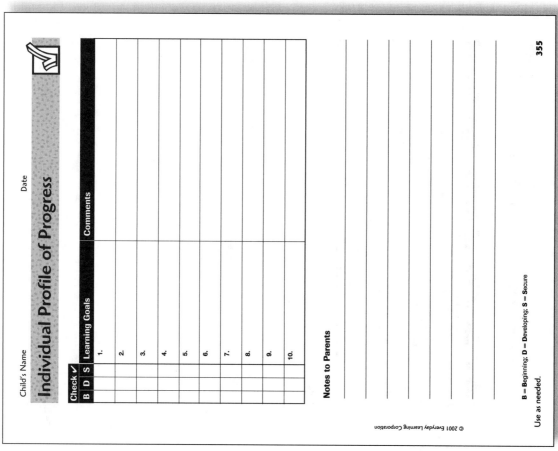

Check ✔

B	D	S	Learning Goals	Comments
			1.	
			2.	
			3.	
			4.	
			5.	
			6.	
			7.	
			8.	
			9.	
			10.	

Notes to Parents

B = Beginning; **D** = Developing; **S** = Secure

Use as needed.

355

Class Progress Indicator

Mathematical Topic Being Assessed: _____

	BEGINNING	DEVELOPING OR DEVELOPING+	SECURE OR SECURE+
First Assessment After Lesson: _____ Dates included: _____ to _____			
Second Assessment After Lesson: _____ Dates included: _____ to _____			
Third Assessment After Lesson: _____ Dates included: _____ to _____			

Notes _____

Use as needed.

358

Names

1.	1.	1.
2.	2.	2.
3.	3.	3.
4.	4.	4.
5.	5.	5.
6.	6.	6.
7.	7.	7.
8.	8.	8.
9.	9.	9.
10.	10.	10.
11.	11.	11.
12.	12.	12.
13.	13.	13.
14.	14.	14.
15.	15.	15.
16.	16.	16.
17.	17.	17.
18.	18.	18.
19.	19.	19.
20.	20.	20.
21.	21.	21.
22.	22.	22.
23.	23.	23.
24.	24.	24.
25.	25.	25.
26.	26.	26.
27.	27.	27.
28.	28.	28.
29.	29.	29.
30.	30.	30.

Use as needed.

357

Rubric

Beginning (B)

Developing (D)

Secure (S)

Use as needed.

360

Child's Name   Date

Parent Reflections

Use some of the following questions (or your own) and tell us how you see your child progressing in mathematics.

Do you see evidence of your child using mathematics at home?

What do you think are your child's strengths and challenges in mathematics?

Does your child demonstrate responsibility for completing Home Links?

What thoughts do you have about your child's progress in mathematics?

Use as needed.

359

Name _____ Date _____

Math Log A

What did you learn in mathematics this week?

_____
_____
_____
_____
_____
_____
_____
_____
_____
_____
_____

© 2001 Everyday Learning Corporation

Use as needed.

362

Name _____ Date _____

About My Math Class

Draw a face or write the words that show how you feel.

Good   OK   Not so good

1. This is how I feel about math.	**2.** This is how I feel about working with others.	**3.** This is how I feel about working by myself.
4. This is how I feel about number stories.	**5.** This is how I feel about doing Home Links.	**6.** This is how I feel about solving problems.

Circle **yes**, **sometimes**, or **no**.

7. I like to figure things out. I am curious.

    yes   sometimes   no

8. I keep trying even when I don't understand something right away.

    yes   sometimes   no

© 2001 Everyday Learning Corporation

Use as needed.

361

Name Date

Math Log B

Question:

Use as needed. 363

Name Date

Math Log C

Work Box

Tell how you solved
this problem.

364 Use as needed.

Name Date

Math Log C

Work Box

Tell how you solved
this problem.

© 2001 Everyday Learning Corporation

364 Use as needed.

Name _____ Date _____

My Work

This work shows that I can _____

_____

I am still learning to _____

_____

Use as needed.

366

Name _____ Date _____

My Work

This is what I know about _____

_____

_____

_____

Use as needed.

366

Name _____ Date _____

Good Work!

🙂 I like this work because _____

_____

_____

_____

_____

_____

Use as needed.

365

Name _____ Date _____

A Number Story

Unit [ ]

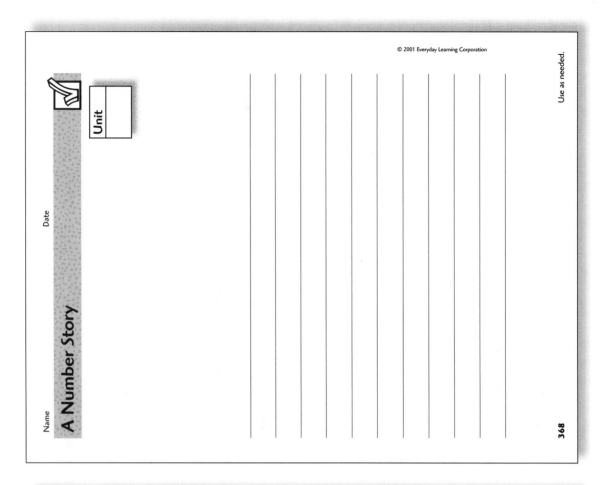

© 2001 Everyday Learning Corporation

Use as needed.

368

Name _____ Date _____

My Exit Slip

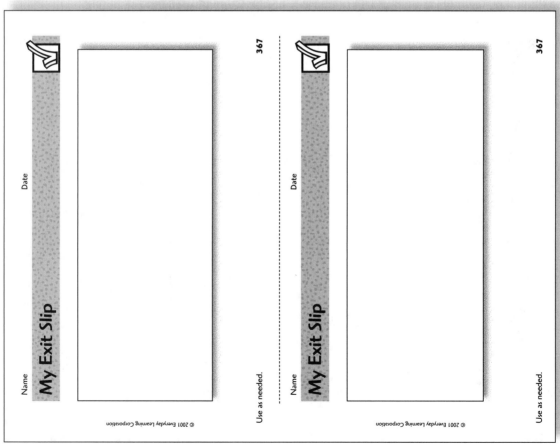

© 2001 Everyday Learning Corporation

Use as needed.

367

Name _____ Date _____

My Exit Slip

© 2001 Everyday Learning Corporation

Use as needed.

367

Name _____ Date _____

"What's My Rule?"

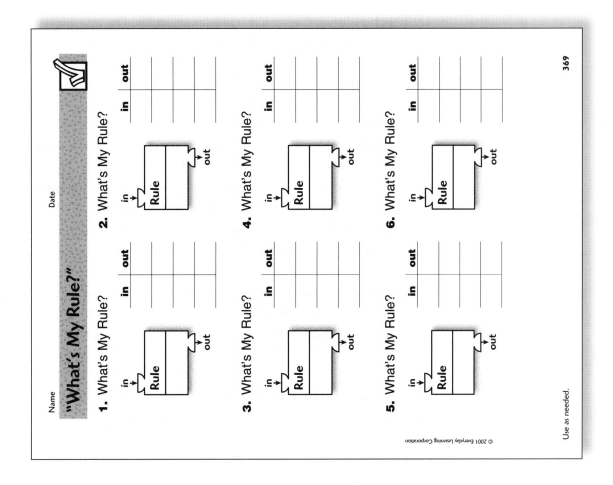

1. What's My Rule?

in	out

in → | Rule | → out

2. What's My Rule?

in	out

in → | Rule | → out

3. What's My Rule?

in	out

in → | Rule | → out

4. What's My Rule?

in	out

in → | Rule | → out

5. What's My Rule?

in	out

in → | Rule | → out

6. What's My Rule?

in	out

in → | Rule | → out

Use as needed.

369

Glossary

assessment The gathering of information about children's progress. This information might include children's knowledge and use of mathematics, as well as their feelings about mathematics. The assessment is used to draw conclusions for individual and class instruction.

assessment sources Mathematical tasks or interactions that can be used for gathering data for assessment purposes.

concepts Basic mathematical ideas that are fundamental in guiding reasoning and problem solving in unfamiliar situations.

evaluation Judgments based on information gathered during assessment.

interviews Conversations between a teacher and individual children during which the teacher can obtain information useful for assessing mathematical progress.

kid-watching The observing and recording of children's interactions and communications during regular instructional activities.

long-term projects Mathematical activities that may require days, weeks, or months to complete.

Mathematics Interest Inventories A written format for assessing children's attitudes toward mathematics.

Math Logs Formats for developing written communication while gathering examples of children's mathematical thinking through writing, pictures, diagrams, and so on.

Ongoing Assessment The gathering of assessment data during regular instructional activities.

open-ended questions Questions that have multiple answers and ways of arriving at these answers. (Open-ended questions are good assessments for problem-solving and reasoning skills.)

outside tests School, district, state, or standardized tests. These tests may or may not match the curriculum.

performance The carrying out or completing of a mathematical activity that displays children's knowledge and judgment while they are engaged in the activity.

Periodic Assessment The more formal gathering of assessment information, often outside of regular instructional time. One example is end-of-unit assessment.

portfolio A sample collection of a child's mathematical work representing his or her progress over the school year.

Product Assessment Samples of children's work, including pictures, diagrams, or concrete representations.

progress The growth, development, and continuous improvement of children's mathematical abilities.

Progress Indicators A form upon which the results of sequential assessment tasks for various mathematical ideas, routines, and concepts can be recorded for the whole class during the school year, using such indicator categories as Beginning, Developing, and Secure.

reflective writing The ability to reflect and write about mathematics, on topics like accomplishments, confidence, feelings, understanding or lack of understanding, goals, and so on.

representative work A piece of work that represents a child's ability and that indicates progress made.

rubric A defined set of guidelines that gives direction for scoring assessment activities. The most useful rubrics are those derived from experience with a wide variety of performances of an assessment task.

self-assessment The ability of children to judge, reflect on, and acknowledge the quality of their mathematical thinking or productions.

standardized tests Typically, nationwide tests that are given, scored, and interpreted in a very consistent way, regardless of the population being tested.

validity of assessment The degree to which assessment data actually represent the knowledge, thought processes, and skills that children have attained.

Index